2 YEAR

Classworks
Literacy

Sara Moult

D1368865

Acknowledgements

The author and publishers wish to thank the following for permission to use copyright material:

Harcourt Education for extracts from Christine Butterworth, *What's Cooking*, Ginn All Aboard, pp. 2–4; Meredith Hooper, *Looking After the Egg*, Ginn All Aboard, pp. 2–3, 10–11; and Peter Haswell, *Putting On a Magic Show*, Ginn All Aboard, pp. 2–3, 14–18;

HarperCollins Publishers for an extract from Jonathan Langley, *Little Red Riding Hood* (1992), pp. 1–17, 22;

David Higham Associates on behalf of the authors for Charles Causley, 'Good Morning, Mr Croco-Doco-Dile' from *Collected Poems for Children* by Charles Causley; and Tony Mitton, 'Puzzled Pea', 'Plum', 'Instructions for Growing Poetry', 'Bubble Songs 1', 'Bubble Songs 2' and 'Mrs Rummage's Muddle-Up Shop' from *Plum* by Tony Mitton, Scholastic (1998);

Libby Houston for 'Shop Chat' from *Cover of Darkness, Selected Poems 1961–1998* by Libby Houston, Slow Dancer Press. Copyright © Libby Houston 1997;

Trevor Millum for 'Dick's Dog';

Judith Nicholls for 'Breakfast for One'. Copyright © 2003 Judith Nicholls;

St Mary's Roman Catholic Primary School, Lowestoft, for 'Autumn Leaves';

The Society of Authors as representative of the Literary Trustees of the author for Walter de la Mare, 'Eeka Neeka', 'The Snowflake', 'Ice', 'Some One', 'Bunches of Grapes', 'Hi!' and 'Done For' from *The Complete Poems of Walter de la Mare* (1969);

Roger Stevens for 'The You Can Be ABC';

Colin West for 'An Alphabet of Horrible Habits';

Walker Books Ltd for extracts from Jill Murphy, *A Quiet Night In* (1996) Copyright © 1996 Jill Murphy.

Shortland Publications for extracts from Fraser Williamson, *Why Frog and Snake Can't Be Friends*, pp 2–18, 21–24.

Every effort has been made to trace the copyright holders but if any have been inadvertently overlooked the publishers will be pleased to make the necessary arrangement at the first opportunity.

Contents

Unit	Outcome	Objectives	Page
Stories with Familiar Settings 1	A story with a familiar setting, focusing on use of connectives to signal time	S1 S2 S4 T6 T10 T11	1
Poetry	A class anthology of poems including original poems modelled on the shared texts	S5 T7 T8 T12	12
Instruction Writing	Instructions (a recipe) for making a sandwich or fruit salad	S2 S4 S6 T13 T14 T16 T17 T18	25
Explanation Texts	A class booklet of explanations about changing materials (linked to QCA Science 'Grouping and changing materials')	S7 T16 T17 T19 T20 T21	42
Information Texts	An information text using questions as headings, with front cover, blurb, sub-headings, captions, labelled diagrams, contents page, introduction and conclusion, in the form of a concertina book	S6 T13 T14 T15 T16 T17 T20	57
Alphabetically Ordered Texts	A glossary and index linked to a current area of study	T16 T17 T18 T20	72
Stories with Familiar Settings 2	A story based on a familiar setting	S3 T3 T10 T11	86
Traditional Tales	A dramatic improvisation of 'Little Red Riding Hood', using finger, sock or stick puppets; own written version of 'Little Red Riding Hood'.	S6 S8 T3 T7	99
Poems by Walter de la Mare	A poem using the structure of a known poem	S2 T8 T9 T10 T11 T15	114
Poems by Tony Mitton	A poem written from initial jottings and words; presentation and performance of own or another poem	S2 T8 T9 T11 T15	133
Poetry with Language Play	A humorous poem	S1 S4 T8 T11	148
Traditional Stories from Other Cultures	A 'traditional' story modelled on the shared text with a change of setting and characters	S3 S5 T3 T4 T5	167

Introduction

How Classworks works

What this book contains

- Chunks of text, both annotated and 'blank' for your own annotations.
- Checklists (or toolkits), planning frames, storyboards, scaffolds and other writing aids.
- Examples of modelled, supported and demonstration writing.
- Lesson ideas including key questions and plenary support.
- Marking ladders for structured self-assessment.
- Blocked unit planning with suggested texts, objectives and outcomes.
- Word-level starter ideas to complement the daily teaching of phonics, handwriting and other skills.
- There are no scripts, no worksheets and nothing you can't change to suit your needs.

How this book is organised

- There are blocked units of work (see previous page) lasting between one week and several, depending on the text type.
- Each blocked unit is organised into a series of chunks of teaching content.
- Each 'chunk' has accompanying checklists and other photocopiable resources.
- For every text we *suggest* annotations, checklists and marking ladders.
- Every unit follows the *teaching sequence for writing* found in *Developing Early Writing* and *Grammar for Writing* (DfES 2001, 2000).
- You can mix and match teaching ideas, units and checklists as you see fit.

How you can use *Classworks* with your medium-term plan

- Refer to your medium-term planning for the blocking of NLS objectives.
- Find the text-type you want to teach (or just the objectives).
- Use the contents page to locate the relevant unit.
- Familiarise yourself with the text and language features using *Classworks* checklists and exemplar analysis pages, and other DfES or QCA resources such as *Grammar for Writing*.
- Browse the lesson ideas and photocopiables to find what you want to use.
- You can just use the text pages ... photocopy and adapt the checklists ... use or change some of the teaching ideas ... take whatever you want and adapt it to fit your class.

Planning a blocked unit of work with Classworks

Classworks units exemplify a blocked unit approach to planning the teaching of Literacy. What follows is an outline of this method of planning and teaching, and how *Classworks* can help you

You need: *Classworks* Literacy Year 2, medium-term planning; OHT (optional).
Optional resources: your own choice of texts for extra analysis; *Grammar for Writing*.

Method

- From the medium-term planning, identify the **outcome**, **texts** and **objectives** you want to teach.

- *Classworks* units **exemplify** how some units could be planned, resourced and taught.

- Decide how to 'chunk' the text you are analysing, for example, introductory paragraph, paragraph 1, paragraph 2, closing paragraph.

- *Classworks* units give an example of **chunking** with accompanying resources and exemplar analysis. Texts for pupil analysis (labelled 'Pupil copymaster') are intended for whole-class display on OHT.

- **Whatever you think of the checklists provided, analyse the text with *your* class and build *your own* checklist for the whole text, and for each chunk.**

- Plan your blocked unit based on the following teaching sequence for writing.

- *Classworks* units outline one way of planning a **blocked unit**, with exemplifications of some days, and suggestions for teaching content on others.

Shared Reading – analysing the text – create 'checklist' or writer's toolkit	The children analyse another of that text type and add to checklist	Review checklist
Shared Writing – demonstrate application of 'checklist' to a small piece of writing	The children write independently based on your demonstration	Use examples on OHT to check against the 'checklist'

- This model is only a guideline, allowing the writing process to be scaffolded. You would want to build in opportunities for planning for writing, talking for writing, teaching explicit word-level and sentence-level objectives that would then be modelled in the shared writing, and so on. There are ideas for word-level and sentence-level starters on pages 182–4.

- Allow opportunities for the children to be familiar with the text type. This might include reading plenty of examples, drama, role play, video, and so on.

Assessment

- Make sure that 'checklists' are displayed around the room and referred to before writing and when assessing writing in the **plenary**.

- One or two children could work on an OHT, which could be the focus of the plenary.

- Use a **marking ladder** for the children to evaluate their writing. This is based on the checklist your class has built up. We give you an example of how it might look for each blocked unit. There's a blank copy on page 185.

What each page does

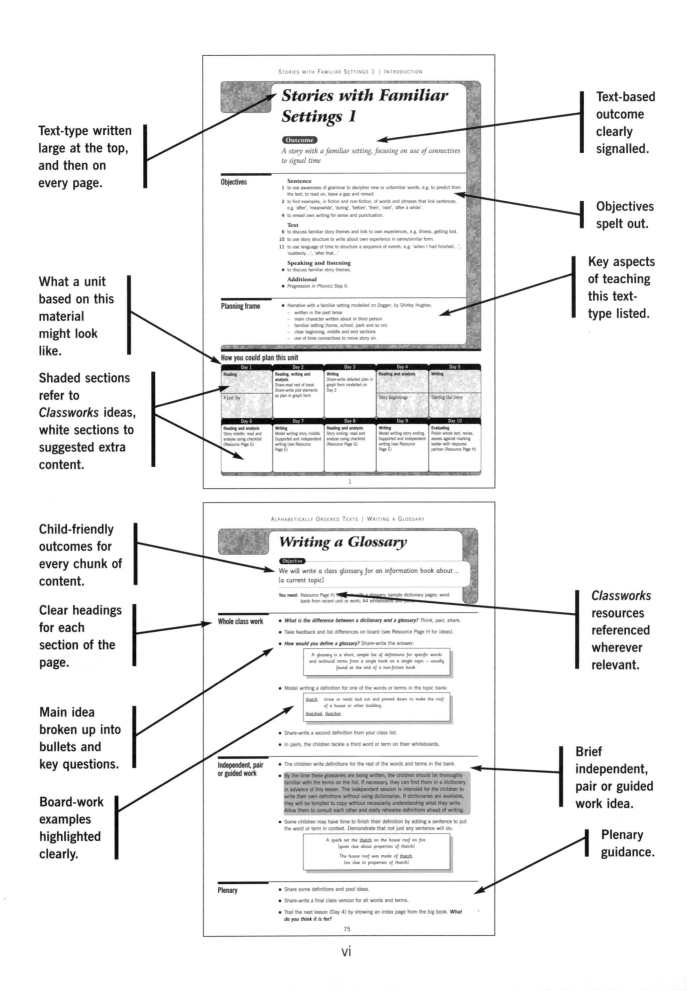

Text-type written large at the top, and then on every page.

Text-based outcome clearly signalled.

Objectives spelt out.

Key aspects of teaching this text-type listed.

What a unit based on this material might look like.

Shaded sections refer to *Classworks* ideas, white sections to suggested extra content.

Child-friendly outcomes for every chunk of content.

Clear headings for each section of the page.

Main idea broken up into bullets and key questions.

Board-work examples highlighted clearly.

Classworks resources referenced wherever relevant.

Brief independent, pair or guided work idea.

Plenary guidance.

Stories with Familiar Settings 1

Outcome

A story with a familiar setting, focusing on use of connectives to signal time

Objectives

Sentence

1 to use awareness of grammar to decipher new or unfamiliar words, e.g. to predict from the text; to read on, leave a gap and reread.

2 to find examples, in fiction and non-fiction, of words and phrases that link sentences, e.g. 'after', 'meanwhile', 'during', 'before', 'then', 'next', 'after a while'.

4 to reread own writing for sense and punctuation.

Text

6 to discuss familiar story themes and link to own experiences, e.g. illness, getting lost.

10 to use story structure to write about own experience in same/similar form.

11 to use language of time to structure a sequence of events, e.g. 'when I had finished...', 'suddenly...', 'after that...'

Speaking and listening

● to discuss familiar story themes.

Additional

● *Progression in Phonics* Step 6.

Planning frame

● Narrative with a familiar setting modelled on *Dogger*, by Shirley Hughes:
  – written in the past tense
  – main character written about in third person
  – familiar setting (home, school, park and so on)
  – clear beginning, middle and end sections
  – use of time connectives to move story on.

How you could plan this unit

Day 1	Day 2	Day 3	Day 4	Day 5
Reading	Reading, writing and analysis Share-read rest of book. Share-write plot elements as plan in graph form	Writing Share-write detailed plan in graph form modelled on Day 2	Reading and analysis	Writing
A Lost Toy			*Story Beginnings*	*Starting Our Story*

Day 6	Day 7	Day 8	Day 9	Day 10
Reading and analysis Story middle: read and analyse using checklist (Resource Page F)	**Writing** Model writing story middle. Supported and independent writing (see Resource Page D)	**Reading and analysis** Story ending: read and analyse using checklist (Resource Page F)	**Writing** Model writing story ending. Supported and independent writing (see Resource Page E)	**Evaluating** Polish whole text, revise, assess against marking ladder with response partner (Resource Page G)

A Lost Toy

Objectives

We will segment to spell words and blend to read words. We will read about a boy who loses his cuddly toy, and talk about losing a favourite cuddly toy

You need: big book version of *Dogger*, by Shirley Hughes; flip chart, whiteboards, pens.

Whole class work

- Play *Progression in Phonics* games using the following words, most of which will be met in today's text: 'read', 'speak', 'teeth', 'real', 'sleep', 'feet', 'field'.

- Introduce the big book *Dogger*. Discuss the front cover and the blurb on the back:
  - *What can we learn from the cover?*
  - *Is this book fiction or non-fiction? What is the difference?*
  - *What do you think we will find inside?*
  - *What is the blurb for?*

- Discuss the theme of a lost toy. ***Do you think the boy will find his toy? Why?***

- Engage the children actively in discussion. Ask open questions to get them thinking; avoid naming a child before asking a question; use *Think, Pair, Share* to involve everyone instead of hands-up; build on their responses to develop a dialogue.

Independent, pair or guided work

- Ask the children to think of their own favourite cuddly toy. ***Has anyone ever lost their toy, even for a short time?***

- In pairs, the children take turns to tell each other about their favourite cuddly toy. You could use these prompts:
  - *What is the toy's name?*
  - *Where did it come from and how long have you had it?*
  - *Why is it special to you?*
  - *What games do you play with it?*
  - *Has it ever been lost?*
  - *How did/would you feel when/if it was lost?*
  - *How did/would you feel when/if it was found again?*

- Encourage the children to ask each other questions to find out more. Some will have exciting, sad, funny or surprising stories to tell. Don't ask them to write anything at this stage – the talk is groundwork, generating ideas for the written outcome.

- Support a discussion pair, encouraging the children to 'embroider' their account to make a better story. This helps the children to see the difference between truth and story-telling, encouraging them to think and talk like writers, who often use personal experience as a starting point for creating narrative.

Plenary

- Revisit lesson objectives: do the children feel they have met them?

- Ask one or two children to recount their partner's experience. Allow the child who told the story to respond, saying whether their partner told it well. This focuses the children's listening and allows you to assess their skills. Listening skills develop through regularly working in this way with a variety of talking partners.

- Read the first three pages of the big book together.

Story Beginnings

Objectives

We will look for time phrases that move the story on. We will put words in a sentence in order. We will also put sentences from the text in order and reread our own writing for sense

You need: big book version of *Dogger*, by Shirley Hughes; Resource Pages A and F; OHTs, flip chart and marker pens; beginnings of other stories with similar themes, for example, *Little Teddy Left Behind*; *Small*; *Where Are You, Blue Kangaroo?*, coloured pencils and highlighters.

Whole class work

- Choose three sentences from Dogger, put them into a word processor and print in large type. Cut up the sentences and give each child a word. Challenge them to find their sentence 'team' and sequence the words together. Each team comes to the front in turn to put their complete sentence on the 'washing line' and read it to the rest of the class. The sentences can then be sequenced by discussion and consensus. 'Get up and go' is a good activity for kinaesthetic learners – they like to be on the move, handling the words and getting themselves into the right order.

- Read, analyse and annotate the beginning of the story.
  - *Why do you think the writer introduces the toy before the child?*
  - *Can you spot a three anywhere?* Answer: three ways Dave plays with Dogger; three preferred toys. *Why do you think the writer puts things in threes?*
  - *What tense are the verbs in?*
  - *Is Dave telling the story?*

  This last question is key as the children will later be drawing on their own experiences, perhaps putting their own toy in the story, but writing in the third person. Lapses into first person are easy, so flag up the third person narrative for them frequently.

- Build a class checklist from the annotations (see Resource Page F for ideas).

Independent, pair or guided work

- In pairs, the children read and annotate the beginning of other 'lost' stories, looking for features found on the checklist and any different ones, including time words and phrases. Photocopies can be annotated using coloured pencils and highlighter pens. Features could be reordered on a simple grid with book titles at the top and *Dogger* features already filled in.

- Your guided group read and annotate their story beginning and develop the checklist.

- *What differences are there between* **Dogger** *and this story? Why do you think this is?*

- *Which story would you most like to read all through? Why?*

Plenary

- *What new time words and phrases emerged from your independent work?* Add these to the class collection.

- Hold up a series of cards with time words and phrases for sentence beginnings (Resource Page A). Working in pairs on whiteboards, the children plan, orally rehearse, write and read for sense suitable endings. Share sentences with the class.

- Trail tomorrow's lesson (writing own story beginning) by inviting the children to bring their own soft toys to 'star' in their stories.

Starting Our Story

Objective

We will write a beginning for a story about a lost toy

You need: Resource Pages B and C; children's own soft toys to 'star' in their stories; teacher's own soft toy for modelled writing; whiteboards and pens.

Whole class work

- *Today we are going to use everything that we have learnt from reading the beginning of the Dogger story to help us write our own story start. Our toys are going to be the 'stars' of the stories, and will help us remember about good story writing.*

- Refer back to the beginning of *Dogger*, which the class read in the previous lesson. Challenge the children, in pairs, to remember the seven points from the checklist: verbs in the past tense; description of toy; written in third person; time phrases to move the story on; introduce family members; how the child plays with the toy; how the toy is lost.

- Refer back to the checklist to find any missing points.

- Using the modelled writing (Resource Page B) as a prompt, demonstrate how to use the style and structure of the story to write your own version of the story start for your own toy. Make it clear that you are only writing the story start today, but are going to write it really carefully, using an author's tricks to make the reader want to read on.

- As you write, verbalise exactly what you are doing and tick off the points on your checklist as you include them.

- Ask the children to read through your modelled version in pairs, and check that you have remembered everything.

- *In pairs, describe to your partner your soft toy and why it is special. How would you feel if you lost it?*

- *On whiteboards, note down the name of your character and the name of your toy. Decide how the toy will get lost, and note that down too. This will act as a story start planner.*

Independent, pair or guided work

- The children write their own versions of a story start about a lost toy, using the class checklist and the planning notes on their whiteboards to focus composition.

- Support lower-achieving children with a writing frame to guide their writing, based on Resource Page C.

Plenary

- The children bring their story starts and read them to their soft toys. The soft toys need to come to life, listening attentively and nodding approvingly!

- In pairs, the children challenge the soft toys to tell each other what they liked about their owner's story start, and whether they noticed anything that had been left out.

(Pupil copymaster)

Time connectives

Once

Sometimes

Now and again

When it was

One afternoon

Just then

On the way home

At tea-time

When Dad came home

At bed-time

Then

The next day

At that moment

When

At last

Right away

That night

(Exemplar material)

Modelled writing

Story beginning – introducing the toy and the child

Once there was a furry grey toy called Ellie. One of her tusks was missing and the other was grubby from cuddling. Her tusk was missing because she had been chewed by the dog when he was a puppy. Ellie belonged to Alex. Alex loved Ellie, and took her to bed, to breakfast and to school, hidden at the bottom of her backpack.

One morning on the way to school Alex took Ellie out to show her the diggers scooping soil on the building site. Mum hurried Alex and her brother Ben along the road towards the school gate just as the bell began to ring.

Story middle – showing how sad the child is, using time phrases as sentence beginnings

At tea-time Alex seemed a bit sad. In the bath she was very quiet and not splashy at all. At bed-time she said: "I want Ellie." But Ellie was nowhere to be found. Alex tried very hard not to cry. Mum looked in the washing basket, to see if Ellie had got mixed up with the washing. Ben hunted in the big wooden toybox in the bedroom. When Dad came home, he went out to the garden and searched in the playhouse. But Ellie was quite lost.

Story end – finding the lost toy and a happy ending

The next day was Saturday and they all went for a walk to the park. On the way, they passed the Post Office with its dusty displays in the window. There, at the very back, was a notice written on yellow card that said

Found. Toy elephant. Please phone 01872 020934

Alex couldn't believe her eyes! She pulled at Mum's hand and dragged her to the window. Mum rushed inside to speak to the shopkeeper, who gave her the address of the lady who had left the card. At once, Mum and Alex found the house and rang the doorbell. A lady answered the door, and hiding behind her legs was a little boy cuddling –

ELLIE!

Alex held out her hand to reach Ellie, but the little boy just held on tighter. Mum asked the little boy if they could please have Ellie back but he shouted: "NO!"

Then Ben did something very kind. He showed the little boy his yellow digger with the moving bucket. The little boy smiled and swapped Ellie for the yellow digger. Alex was so happy she gave Ben a very big hug.

"Thank you, Ben," she said.

Classworks Literacy Year 2 © Sara Moult, Nelson Thornes Ltd 2003

(Pupil copymaster)

Writing frame 1

Story beginning – introducing the toy and the child.

Once there was a _____

toy called _____ . One of

_____

and the other _____

_____ .

_____ was missing

because _____

_____ .

_____ belonged to

_____ .

(Pupil copymaster)

Writing frame 2

Story middle – showing how sad the child is, using time phrases as sentence beginnings.

At tea-time _____

_____ .

In the bath _____

_____ .

At bed-time _____ said:

"I want _____ ."

But _____ was nowhere

to be found.

Writing frame 3

Story end – finding the lost toy and a happy ending.

The next day was _____

and they all went _____

_____ . There,

at the very back, was _____ .

But the little _____

_____ .

Then _____ did

something very kind. He _____

_____ .

"Thank you _____ ," said

_____ .

(Exemplar material)

Checklists for stories with familiar settings

Example of a checklist for a story beginning ①

- Use verbs in the past tense
- Include a description of the toy
- Write about child in the third person
- Begin sentences with time phrases to move the story on: 'Sometimes', 'Now and again'
- Introduce other family members
- List a few ways the child likes to play with the toy
- Describe how the toy is lost

Example of a checklist for a story middle ②

- Use verbs in the past tense
- Write about child in the third person
- Use verbs 'looked', 'searched', 'hunted'
- Use phrases 'nowhere to be found', 'quite lost'
- Describe three of the child's actions to show feelings
- Three people look for the toy – interesting places
- Describe child's action to show how toy is missed

Example of a checklist for a story ending ③

- Use verbs in the past tense
- Write about child in the third person
- Use exciting verbs when toy is seen: 'rushed', 'hurried'
- Use exclamation marks after exciting sentences
- Try to use 'at once', 'quickly', 'at last'
- Include change of setting
- Include child's actions to show feelings
- Introduce a new character outside the family, helpful or unhelpful
- Describe three tries to get the toy back, third one works
- Describe child's action to show happiness

Marking ladder

Name: _____

Pupil	Objective	Teacher
	I used verbs in the past tense.	
	I wrote a description of the toy.	
	I wrote about the child in the third person.	
	I began sentences with time phrases to move the story on: 'Sometimes', 'Now and again'.	
	I used the verbs 'looked', 'searched', 'hunted'.	
	I used the phrases 'nowhere to be found', 'quite lost'.	
	I used exciting verbs when the toy was seen: 'rushed', 'hurried'.	
	I used exclamation marks after exciting sentences.	
	I tried to use 'at once', 'quickly', 'at last'.	
	I included a change of setting.	
	What could I do to improve my story next time?	

Poetry

Outcome

A class anthology of poems including original poems modelled on the shared texts

Objectives

Sentence

5 to revise knowledge about other uses of capitalisation, e.g. for names, headings, titles, emphasis, and begin to use in own writing.

Text

7 to learn, reread and recite favourite poems, taking account of punctuation; to comment on aspects such as word combinations, sound patterns (such as rhymes, rhythms, alliterative patterns) and forms of presentation.

8 to collect and categorise poems to build class anthologies.

12 to use simple poetry structures and to substitute own ideas, write new lines.

Planning frame

- Read poems and analyse structure and features.
- Use poems as a planning frame for writing own poems.

How you could plan this unit

Day 1	Day 2	Day 3	Day 4	Day 5
Reading and analysis	Writing	Reading and analysis Read poem *Autumn Leaves* (Resource Page E) and identify text features. Make a checklist (see Resource Page H for ideas). Annotate first stanza together using checklist (Resource Page F)	Writing	Writing and performing Independent writing of final stanza. Performance of finished poems. Evaluate using marking ladder (Resource Page I)
Alliteration 1	*Alliteration 2*		*Choosing Words*	

12

Alliteration 1

Objectives

We will recite favourite poems taking account of punctuation, and noticing alliteration and sound patterns. We will collect and categorise poems including alliteration to add to our anthology

You need: Resource Pages A–C.

Whole class work

- Explain that today you are going to read some poems about children. Read together *Bullying Bertha* (Resource Page A). ***Do you notice anything about the words that the author has chosen? Sometimes poets choose to put words next to each other which start with the same letter or sound. This is called 'alliteration' and it's a useful tool in the poet's tool box.***

- Identify the alliteration in *Bullying Bertha*, for example 'pushes, pinches and pulls' and 'burps and belches'. Explain that alliteration can help the rhythm of a poem.

- The children may have heard alliteration before in tongue-twisters. Have some fun trying one or two such as:

> Wayne went to Wales to watch walruses
>
> Seven slimey snakes slowly sliding south
>
> Four furious friends fought for the phone

- Tell the children the next poem is about when they grow up. Read aloud *The You Can Be A B C* (Resource Page B) and check that the children understand some of the more difficult vocabulary. Ask for volunteers to come to the front and circle the alliterative words. Point out that it is also an alphabet poem.

Independent, pair or guided work

- Give the children the poem *Inside the Classroom* (Resource Page C). Working in pairs, ask them to find all the examples of alliteration and to practise saying the poem aloud to each other. ***Listen for the similar sounds when it is spoken aloud by your partner.***

Plenary

- Review the alliterative words found in *Inside the Classroom*. Point out that sometimes alliteration can be found in words which have the same sound rather than the same letter at the beginning. Look at the line 'Clever Chris kicking coins across the carpet'. Point out the alliteration in 'Chris' and 'across'.

- Ask each child to try to think of an alliterative word to go with their own name. Try these around the class.

Alliteration 2

Objectives

We will use simple poetry structures and substitute our own ideas to write new lines. We will write a shared poem using alliteration for the class anthology

You need: Resource Page D; strips of paper.

Whole-class work

- Select a group of six to eight children. Using the alliterative names they invented in the previous lesson's plenary, play 'Let's introduce the class'. Sitting in a circle, the first child says, 'Welcome to Class 2, I am Brave Ben.' The next child in the circle adds, 'Welcome to Class 2, he is Brave Ben and I am Handsome Harrison.' Child 3 says, 'Welcome to Class 2, he is Brave Ben, he is Handsome Harrison and I am Lovely Lydia.' Continue in this way all the way around the circle. You then try to call out everybody's name.

- Explain that they will be able to use their alliterative names in today's poem.

- Read aloud *An Alphabet of Horrible Habits* (Resource Page D). Explain that they are going to write pairs of lines to make an alphabet poem about their own class.

- Use the first two lines of the poem as a model. This will work best if you substitute names from your own class and alter the descriptions accordingly, for example:

  > A is for Amiable Annie who never makes a noise
  >
  > B is for Bossy Beth who bullies the boys

- As you work point out:
  - each line follows the structure 'A is for _____ [adjective] _____ [child's name] who _____ [add own phrase]
  - the rhyme 'noise' and 'boys'. Explain that rhyming is sometimes difficult – the children should not worry about making their own lines rhyme
  - each line should use at least one example of alliteration, for example 'Amiable Annie'
  - some lines may have more alliteration, for example 'Bossy Beth bullies boys'.

- Choose another pair of children and scribe a pair of lines from class suggestions.

Independent, pair or guided work

- Organise the children to work with a partner whose first name is alphabetically adjacent to their own.

- The children write their two lines of the poem on strips of paper. Encourage them to say the lines aloud to decide if they work well.

- Some children might join up with another pair to read and listen to four lines working together.

Plenary

- Help the children to organize themselves alphabetically. Then each child reads aloud their line in order. Carefully collect the strips of paper in order and read the poem to the children. ***Which lines work very well? Do any not fit? Can they be changed slightly to work better?***

14

Choosing Words

Objective

We will write a poem modelled on *Autumn Leaves*, starting each line with a capital letter

You need: Resource Pages E–H; flip chart and marker pens; whiteboards and pens.

Whole class work

- Using Resource Page E and the examplar analysis (Resource Page F) for reference, explain that the children are going to use the format of this poem to help them write their own version called *Assembly Children*.

- Establish how many stanzas the shared poem will need by identifying key aspects of the experience, for example, being quiet, singing, praying, and so on.

- Use *Think, Pair, Share* to refresh the children's memories of what happens when they leave their classroom and arrive and settle at the assembly hall. Scribe a list of appropriate verbs from their suggestions.

- Write these on the board. Agree on a noun phrase to begin and end the stanza.

- Demonstrate writing the first stanza (Resource Page G), modelling choosing and grouping the verbs for maximum effect, orally rehearsing lines, editing and commenting as you write.

- Agree a noun phrase for the second stanza and use *Think, Pair, Share* to produce a second verb collection to scribe.

Independent, pair or guided work

- In pairs, the children write the middle lines of the second stanza, choosing, grouping and orally rehearsing the verbs into lines as demonstrated.

Plenary

- Revisit the lesson objectives.

- In pairs, the children use the class checklist (see Resource Page H for ideas) to evaluate their partner's stanzas. **Has everyone remembered to start each line with a capital letter?**

- Select one of the children's examples and read both stanzas aloud. **Do they sound as though they belong together?**

- The children comment using a response sandwich: one good comment; one area for improvement; another good comment.

(**Pupil copymaster**)

Bullying Bertha

In the playground she pushes, pinches and pulls,

Naughty and nasty – not nice to know.

She bounces the boys to and fro

And trips the girls over;

She even burps and belches, when it is time to go.

The You Can Be ABC

You can be
an artistic actor or a brainy barrister
a clever conductor or a dynamic dancer
an evil enemy or a fantastic friend
a green-fingered gardener or a healing herbalist
an interesting inventor or a jovial jolly juggler
a keen kitchen designer or a loggerheaded lumberjack
a melodious musician or a natty newsreader
an over-the-top opera singer or a princely-paid pop star
a quipping quiz master or a rugged rugby player
a serious scientist or a typewriting traveller
an uppity umpire or a vigorous vet
a wonderful winner or an expert xylophonist
a yelling yachtsperson or a zealous zoologist.
So go to it, you can do it.
Someone's got to, why not you?
And who is going to stop you?
The only person who can stop you –
that's YOU

Roger Stevens, in The Works, *poems chosen by Paul Cookson*

(Pupil copymaster)

Inside the Classroom

Inside the classroom
there is:

Angry Abigail eating appetizing apples

Bertha Barnes blowing big, blue bubbles

Clever Chris kicking coins across the carpet

Dwayne Dwiddle drawing dreaded Dracula

Elmer Elwood enchanting eleven elderly elephants

French Freddie feeding ferocious fish

Greedy Gilbert growling at giggly girls
whilst

Tanya Tatters, the teacher, takes tea and toast!

An Alphabet of Horrible Habits

A is for Albert who makes lots of noise
B is for Bertha who bullies the boys
C is for Cuthbert who teases the cat
D is for Dilys whose singing is flat
E is for Enid who's never on time
F is for Freddy who's covered in slime
G is for Gilbert who never says thanks
H is for Hannah who plans to rob banks
I is for Ivy who slams the front door
J is for Jacob whose jokes are a bore
K is for Kenneth who won't wash his face
L is for Lucy who cheats in a race
M is for Maurice who gobbles his food
N is for Nora who runs about nude
O is for Olive who treads on your toes
P is for Percy who picks his nose
Q is for Queenie who won't tell the truth
R is for Rupert who's rather uncouth
S is for Sibyl who bellows and bawls
T is for Thomas who scribbles on walls
U is for Una who fidgets too much
V is for Victor who talks double Dutch
W is for Wilma who won't wipe her feet
X is for Xerxes who never is neat
Y is for Yorick who's vain as can be
And Z is for Zoe who doesn't love me.

Colin West, in The Works, *poems chosen by Paul Cookson*

(Pupil copymaster)

Autumn Leaves

Autumn leaves.
Shrivelling, shivering, shaking.
Floating, fluttering,
Flapping, flying, falling.
Rustling, rattling,
Cluttering, crunching.

Break-time children.
Screaming, scrunching, shouting.
Cleaning, clearing, cackling.
Giggling, gathering, grabbing,
Stuffing down necks.
Screeching, scratching.
Kicking, flinging, catching.

Duty teacher.
Whistle-blowing, finger-wagging.
Frowning, pointing, stopping.
Bossing, bothering, boiling.
Grumping, growling,
Giving up!
Laughing teacher –
Autumn leaves.

St Mary's RC Primary School, Lowestoft, Suffolk

Classworks Literacy Year 2 © Sara Moult, Nelson Thornes Ltd 2003

Example of analysis of *Autumn Leaves*

First line repeats the noun phrase (poem's subject).

Alliteration (examples underlined).

Three noun phrases.

All lines begin with capital letters.

Poem ends with two noun phrases.

Autumn leaves.
<u>Sh</u>rivelling, <u>sh</u>ivering, <u>sh</u>aking.
<u>F</u>loating, <u>fl</u>uttering,
<u>F</u>lapping, <u>fl</u>ying, <u>f</u>alling.
<u>R</u>ustling, <u>r</u>attling,
<u>C</u>luttering, <u>c</u>runching.

Break-time children.
<u>Scr</u>eaming, <u>scr</u>unching, <u>sh</u>outing.
<u>C</u>leaning, <u>c</u>learing, <u>c</u>ackling.
<u>G</u>iggling, <u>g</u>athering, <u>g</u>rabbing,
Stuffing down necks.
<u>Scr</u>eeching, <u>scr</u>atching.
Kicking, flinging, catching.

Duty teacher.
Whistle-blowing, finger-wagging.
Frowning, pointing, stopping.
<u>B</u>ossing, <u>b</u>othering, <u>b</u>oiling.
<u>G</u>rumping, <u>g</u>rowling,
<u>G</u>iving up!
Laughing teacher –
Autumn leaves.

St Mary's RC Primary School, Lowestoft, Suffolk

Title is noun phrase.

List of verbs.

Non-finite ending repeats.

Pattern repeats: verbs are clustered in twos, threes or fours.

Double-barrelled (conjoined) adjectives (built from non-finite verbs).

The last line is the first line/ title repeated.

(Pupil copymaster)

Modelled writing

Assembly children.

Paper-flapping, forgetting.

Sniffing, stuttering, stumbling.

Blushing, throat-clearing, remembering.

Speaking up, smiling, sitting down.

Assembly children.

(Exemplar material)

Checklist for poetry

- Each stanza begins and ends with a noun phrase

- Title is first noun phrase

- Non-finite verbs ('-ing' words) are used

- Verbs are listed in threes, fours or fives using some alliteration

- Each line begins with a capital letter

- Final stanza has an extra line that is also poem's title and has a full stop

Marking ladder

Name: _____

Pupil	Objective	Teacher
	I began and ended each stanza with a noun phrase.	
	I used the title as the first noun phrase.	
	I used non-finite verbs, listed in groups.	
	I used alliteration.	
	I began each line with a capital letter.	
	I wrote an extra line for the final stanza that is also the poem's title	
	I used a full stop at the end of the last line.	
	What could I do to improve my poem next time?	

Instruction Writing

Outcome

Instructions (a recipe) for making a sandwich or fruit salad

Objectives

Sentence

2 to find examples, in fiction and non-fiction, of words and phrases that link sentences, e.g. 'after', 'meanwhile', 'during', 'before', 'then', 'next', 'after a while'.

4 to reread own writing for sense and punctuation.

6 to use a variety of simple organisational devices, e.g. arrows, lines, boxes, keys, to indicate sequences and relationships.

Text

13 to read simple written instructions in the classroom, simple recipes, plans, instructions for constructing something.

14 to note key structural features, e.g. clear statement of purpose at start, sequential steps set out in a list, direct language.

16 to use models from reading to organise instructions sequentially, e.g. listing points in order, each point depending on the previous one, numbering.

17 to use diagrams in instructions, e.g. drawing and labelling diagrams as part of a set of instructions.

18 to use appropriate register in writing instructions, i.e. direct, impersonal, building on texts read.

Planning frame

- Read examples of instructions for different tasks.

- Annotate and use to write own instructions.

Notes

- To follow up this unit, the children could make a food or craft item at home, write the instructions independently using the checklist and bring the results to school for display. Collate their sets of instructions into a class book.

- Don't overlook the potential for spoofs – children enjoy writing instructions for winding up Mum or producing the perfect Saturday!

- This unit can be linked to Design Technology. To help the children write clear instructions it is important that these should relate to a real, current experience. A hands-on approach is taken throughout, with instructions emerging from actions.

How you could plan this unit

Day 1	Day 2	Day 3	Day 4	Day 5
Reading and analysis The children bring examples of instructions from home for classroom display. Introduce text, identify text type. Skim-read contents and headings	**Reading and analysis** Read and annotate introduction and 'You will need' list using checklist (see Resource Page L for ideas). Independent annotation of text	**Reading and writing** Attempt to follow faulty instructions and share-write instructions	**Reading and analysis** *Main Features*	**Writing** Demonstration writing of another set of instructions (based on Resource Pages A–D). The children share-write or are supported to write an introduction and 'You will need' list for, for example, a DT task

Day 6	Day 7	Day 8	Day 9	Day 10
Applying instructions *Sequencing Steps*	**Writing** Demonstrate writing a concluding statement for the instructions written on Day 6. The children independently write their own instructions	**Reading and analysis** Read instructions that include a divided list and sequencing words. Adapt checklist using terms 'equipment' and 'materials' or 'ingredients'. Can the children identify the difference?	**Apply** Demonstrate making squash or similar. Share-write instructions	**Writing** The children independently write a divided list and concluding statement for the instructions written on Day 9

Main Features

Objectives

We will put instructions in order. We will also find words like 'after', 'meanwhile', 'during', 'before', 'then', 'next' and 'after a while' in a set of instructions

You need: Resource Pages A–J and L; individual whiteboards; flip chart and marker pens.

Whole-class work

- Read *It's Magic!* (Resource Pages A–D). The children come to the front to ring features for annotation as they arise, for example, heading, sub-headings, diagrams, labels, numbers, imperative verbs, and so on (see Resource Pages E–H).

- Discuss how all these features work together to produce clarity of instruction.

- Read the cloud panel (Resource Page C). Identify the text type as narrative. **What is narrative doing here?** The children discuss answers with response partners, then share with the class.

- Look carefully at instruction 11. **Is it really part of the instructions?** Answer: no, it's the conclusion.

- Produce a class checklist of features from this annotation (see Resource Page L for ideas).

Independent, pair or guided work

- Read and annotate the narrative on making a packed lunch (Resource Page I) which uses terms like 'next', 'then', 'while', 'before', 'after'.

- The children work in pairs to identify and highlight features.
  - *Highlight all the things that would go on a 'You will need' list in one colour.*
  - *Highlight imperative verbs in another colour.*
  - *Write numbers where each instruction starts.*
  - *Cross out unnecessary text in the narrative.*
  - *Change the verbs to imperatives, list and number them on individual whiteboards.*

- Using the checklist, the children turn this or Resource Page J (*What a dirty dog!*) into a set of numbered instructions.

Plenary

- Share some annotated texts from the independent session. Challenge the children to turn them into clearer instructions verbally, one section at a time – heading, 'You will need' list, first instruction.

- *Who can compose an introduction? A conclusion?*

- *Which instructions would be easier to follow?*

Sequencing Steps

Objective

We will make a fruit salad (or similar), using time language to sequence instructions

You need: Resource Page K; materials for making fruit salad for each pair; A4 paper for folding to make a grid; pencils.

Whole class work

- Remind the children that folding paper to make a grid framework is a familiar task.

- Encourage the children to discuss the task with their response partner, including any important reminders.

- Demonstrate folding and unfolding the A4 paper to give a grid framework for diagrams and text.

Independent, pair or guided work

- Each child folds their piece of paper, opens it out and numbers the boxes in the grid 1–6 or 1–8 in the corners.

- The children work in pairs to carry out the task of making a fruit salad (or similar), noting the steps in order and sketching a quick diagram for each step.

- Each pair agree and write a sentence or two of text for each frame of the grid, using the instruction terms (Resource Page K) as sentence beginnings.

- The children read their text to check for sense and meaning.

Plenary

- Ask the children to share the high point of the task – the 'golden moment'.

- Display all the sheets for the whole class to see and celebrate their achievement.

(Pupil copymaster)

It's Magic!

This will show you how to put on a magic show.

You will need:

– a costume...

– a wand...

Cut a piece of dowelling 30cm long. Paint it black with white tips. Add colourful shapes or stickers.

– lots of colourful hankies (or pieces of tissue paper)...

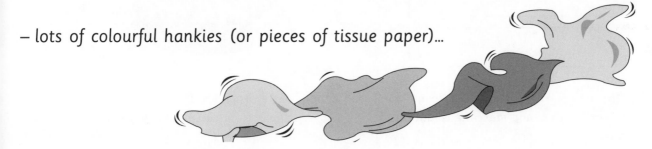

– three card cylinders like these...

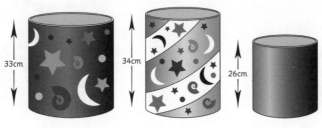

33cm   34cm   26cm

– a wizard's hat, decorated like the cylinders (see next page for instructions on making your own)...

Classworks Literacy Year 2 © Sara Moult, Nelson Thornes Ltd 2003

Pupil copymaster

It's Magic! (2)

– a table covered with a cloth.

You will also need a magic spell. Try this one:

Fizz, Whizz Do the Bizz!

How to make your own wizard's hat

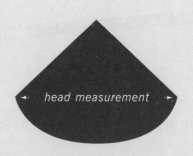

head measurement

1. Measure your head all the way round with a tape measure and mark the length on to a thin piece of card.

2. Cut out a shape like this. Double check that the bottom curve fits your head.

3. Join the sides together with tape to make a cone shape.

4. Decorate the hat with cut-out paper shapes, such as stars and moons.

(**Pupil copymaster**)

It's Magic! (3): getting ready

1. Before the show begins, stand the biggest cylinder on end.

2. Slot the other two cylinders inside it.

3. Fill the smallest cylinder with the hankies.

4. Tell the audience this story:

Once upon a time, the King had a dreadful cold. He sniffled and snuffled. Nobody could help him.

Then a magician called the Wonderful Wiz came to court.

"Oh King," said the Wiz, "I cannot stop your sniffles. But with my magic cylinders I can make you feel better."

This is what he did...

Pupil copymaster

It's Magic! (4): the trick

5. Lift off the first cylinder. Show that it is empty by putting your arm or your wand through it.

6. Slot it back over the second cylinder.

7. Lift out the second cylinder. Show that it is empty.

8. Slot it back into the first cylinder.

9. Say your spell.

Fizz, Whizz Do the Bizz!

10. Reach into the cylinders. Pull out lots of hankies!

11. Make a final bow and thank the audience. **Wait for the applause!**

Classworks Literacy Year 2 © Sara Moult, Nelson Thornes Ltd 2003

(**Exemplar analysis**)

Example of analysis of *It's Magic!*

Heading.

Introduction –
short sentence in
future tense tells
reader purpose of
instructions.

Sub-heading for
list.

Ellipsis shows
'more to come'.

Pictures make a
list.

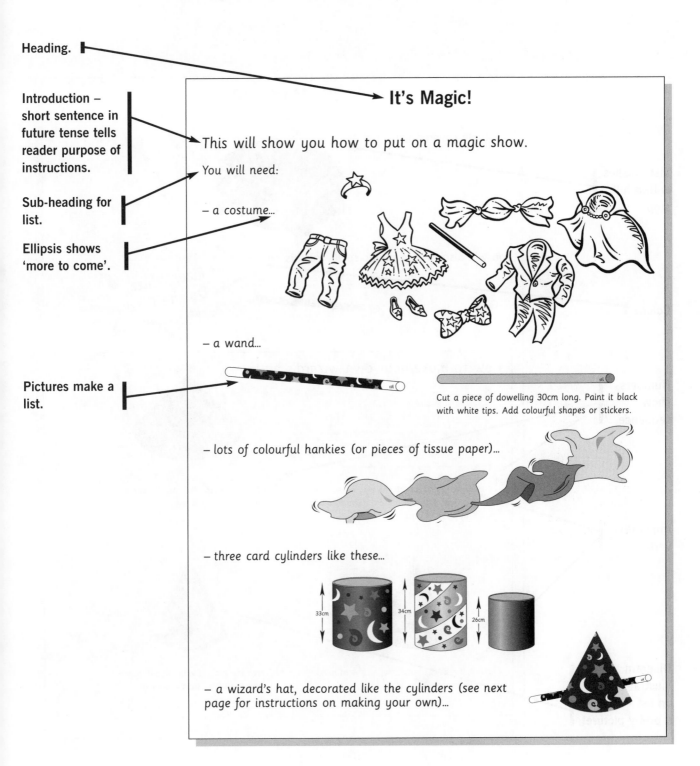

It's Magic!

This will show you how to put on a magic show.

You will need:

– a costume...

– a wand...

Cut a piece of dowelling 30cm long. Paint it black
with white tips. Add colourful shapes or stickers.

– lots of colourful hankies (or pieces of tissue paper)...

– three card cylinders like these...

33cm   34cm   26cm

– a wizard's hat, decorated like the cylinders (see next
page for instructions on making your own)...

Exemplar analysis

Example of analysis of *It's Magic! (2)*

It's Magic! (2)

Continues list.

– a table covered with a cloth.

List finishes with a full stop.

You will also need a magic spell. Try this one:

Colon.

Fizz, Whizz Do the Bizz!

How to make your own wizard's hat

Numbers show sequence.

head measurement

1. Measure your head all the way round with a tape measure and mark the length on to a thin piece of card.

2. Cut out a shape like this. Double check that the bottom curve fits your head.

Imperative verbs.

3. Join the sides together with tape to make a cone shape.

4. Decorate the hat with cut-out paper shapes, such as stars and moons.

Diagram illustrates item on list – not just a pretty picture!

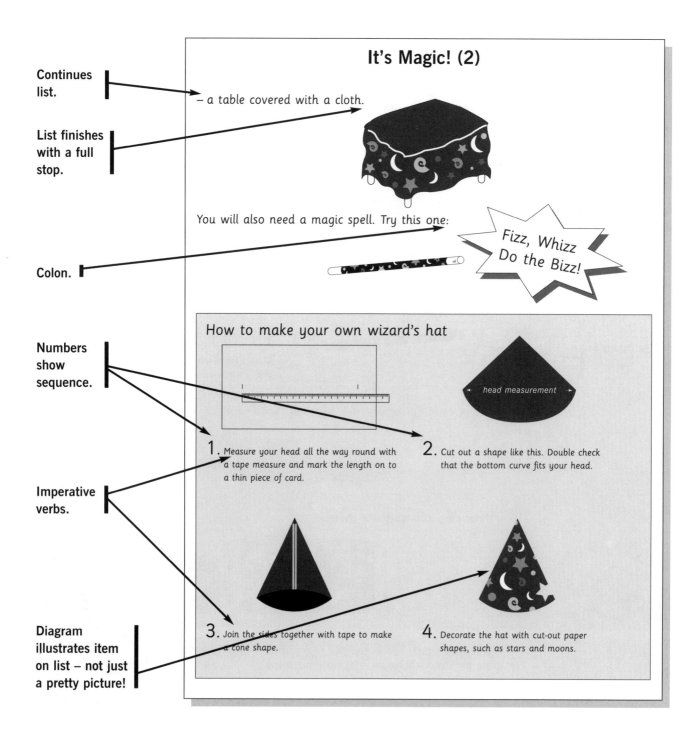

Classworks Literacy Year 2 © Sara Moult, Nelson Thornes Ltd 2003

(Pupil copymaster)

Example of analysis of *It's Magic! (3): getting ready*

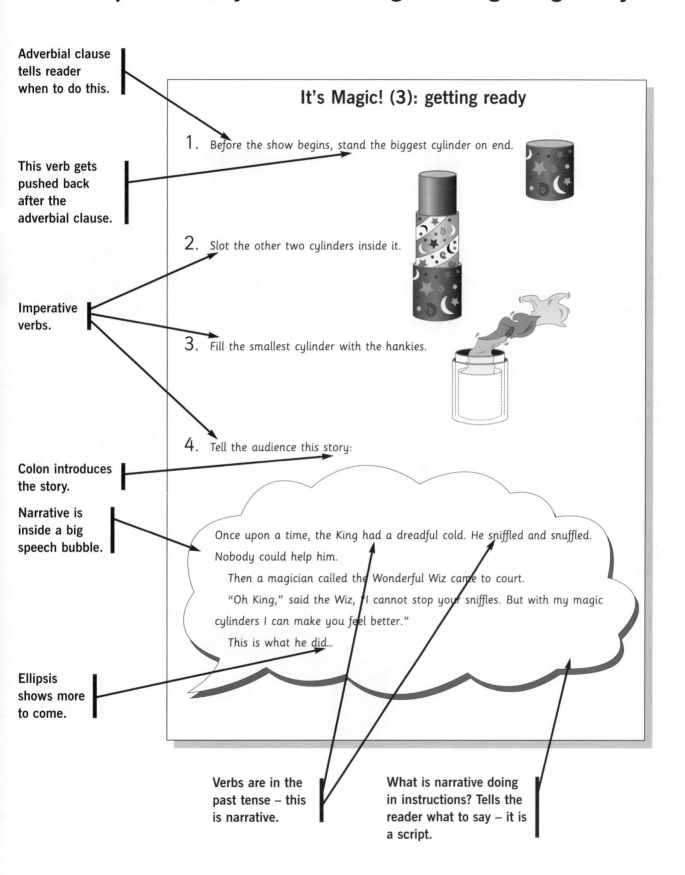

Adverbial clause tells reader when to do this.

This verb gets pushed back after the adverbial clause.

Imperative verbs.

Colon introduces the story.

Narrative is inside a big speech bubble.

Ellipsis shows more to come.

Verbs are in the past tense – this is narrative.

What is narrative doing in instructions? Tells the reader what to say – it is a script.

It's Magic! (3): getting ready

1. Before the show begins, stand the biggest cylinder on end.

2. Slot the other two cylinders inside it.

3. Fill the smallest cylinder with the hankies.

4. Tell the audience this story:

Once upon a time, the King had a dreadful cold. He sniffled and snuffled. Nobody could help him.

Then a magician called the Wonderful Wiz came to court.

"Oh King," said the Wiz, "I cannot stop your sniffles. But with my magic cylinders I can make you feel better."

This is what he did...

Exemplar analysis

Example of analysis of *It's Magic! (4)*

Instructions continue.

Numbers sequence imperative verbs to tell the reader what to do.

Diagrams help reader understand.

Imperative verbs.

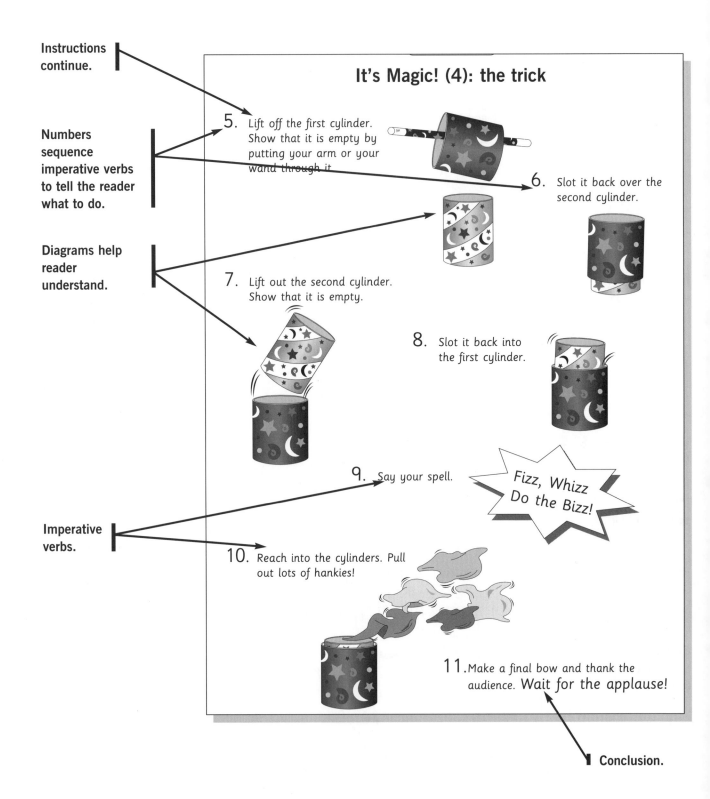

It's Magic! (4): the trick

5. Lift off the first cylinder. Show that it is empty by putting your arm or your wand through it.

6. Slot it back over the second cylinder.

7. Lift out the second cylinder. Show that it is empty.

8. Slot it back into the first cylinder.

9. Say your spell.

Fizz, Whizz Do the Bizz!

10. Reach into the cylinders. Pull out lots of hankies!

11. Make a final bow and thank the audience. Wait for the applause!

Conclusion.

Classworks Literacy Year 2 © Sara Moult, Nelson Thornes Ltd 2003

Pupil copymaster

How to prepare your own packed lunch

Why not pack your own school lunch? The night before, put your boxed drink or plastic bottle of squash in the freezer. This is a good way to keep your lunch fresh and it should be thawed out ready to drink by lunchtime.

In the morning make your sandwich with your favourite filling. Then put it on a board and cut it into two or four pieces. Keep your fingers out of the way of the knife as you cut! Next put the sandwich in a plastic sandwich bag to stop it drying out.

After that, get an apple or orange, a pot of yoghurt, a bag of crisps or anything else you like to have for lunch. Remember, you will need a spoon for your yoghurt. A plastic one is a good idea, so you don't lose the best teaspoons from home.

A piece of cheese makes a healthy part of your lunch but you will need to wrap it in cling film or a piece of foil. If you are allowed a little chocolate bar, get that out too.

Now get your drink out of the freezer and put it in the middle of your lunchbox.

Finally, pack all the other things neatly around the frozen drink and close the lunchbox carefully. After that, you are ready to set off for school. Happy and healthy eating!

Pupil copymaster

What a dirty dog!

When our dog Toby dug a hole in the mud, he got really dirty! Mum said we had to give him a bath and I could help her.

First we got out all the things we needed. Toby had to stay outside for this bit. Mum got his special dog shampoo while I fetched a clean, old towel from the airing cupboard. Then Mum put my old baby bath on the kitchen floor and used a jug to half fill the bath with warm water.

Next it was time to put the dog in the bath. I had to lure him in with one of his favourite bone-shaped biscuits and hold on to his collar to stop him jumping straight out again. Mum squeezed some dog shampoo on his fur and rubbed and scrubbed until all the mud was gone.

After that, we took him outside to rinse him off with the hose while he shook himself and made us wet with the drops. Next I rubbed him all over with the towel. He thought it was a game and tried to play tug of war with me!

Then we took him for a long walk and let him off his lead so he could run around and get dry in the sunshine.

Finally, while Mum emptied the bath and mopped the kitchen floor, I brushed Toby's fur until he looked smart and glossy.

Instruction terms

next

then

while

before

after

(Exemplar material)

Checklist for instruction writing

- Use a 'How to' heading

- Use an introduction to hook the reader

- Include a 'You will need' sub-heading

- List requirements in 1 or 2 lists (equipment/materials)

- Use numbered instructions appropriately sequenced

- Use imperative (bossy) verb in present tense to begin each instruction

- Use impersonal tone (not 'you' or 'I')

- Include diagrams linked to instructions

- Use devices such as labels, arrows, lines and keys

- Write a short conclusion to affirm and/or suggest next action

Marking ladder

Name: _____

Pupil	Objective	Teacher
	I used a 'How to' heading.	
	I used an introduction to hook the reader.	
	I used a 'You will need' sub-heading.	
	I gave requirements in 1 or 2 lists (equipment/materials).	
	I used numbered instructions appropriately sequenced.	
	I used an imperative (bossy) verb in the present tense to begin each instruction.	
	I used an impersonal tone (no 'you' or 'I').	
	I linked diagrams to instructions.	
	I used devices such as labels, arrows, lines and keys.	
	I included a short conclusion to affirm and/or suggest next action.	
	What could I do to improve my instructions next time?	

Explanation Texts

Outcome

*A class booklet of explanations about changing materials
(linked to QCA Science 'Grouping and changing materials')*

Objectives

Sentence

7 to investigate and recognise a range of other ways of presenting texts, e.g. speech bubbles, enlarged, bold or italicised print, captions, headings and sub-headings.

Text

16 to use dictionaries and glossaries to locate words by using initial letter.

17 [be taught] that dictionaries and glossaries give definitions and explanations; discuss what definitions are, explore some simple definitions in dictionaries.

19 to read flow charts and cyclical diagrams that explain a process.

20 to make class dictionaries and glossaries of special interest words, giving explanations and definitions, e.g. linked to topics, derived from stories, poems.

21 to produce simple flow charts or diagrams that explain a process.

Planning frame

- Read and analyse examples of explanation texts.
- Annotate and identify diagrams, headings and captions.
- Write own explanation text based on these features.
- Investigate and write a glossary.
- Discuss and improve work alone or with a partner.

How you could plan this unit

Day 1	Day 2	Day 3	Day 4	Day 5
Reading and analysis Show the children samples of explanation texts. Skim-read cover, contents and headings, identify text type	**Reading and analysis**	**Writing** Produce labelled diagrams and captioned pictures for science observation	**Reading and analysis** Read, annotate and evaluate using checklist	**Apply** Explain the process observed in science observation. Demonstrate writing the opening (Resource Page D)
	Labels and Captions			

Day 6	Day 7	Day 8	Day 9	Day 10
Reading and analysis Read flow diagram (Resource Page E). Annotate using checklist	**Writing**	**Reading and analysis**	**Reading and writing** Build own glossary of terms from science investigation. Investigate a glossary	**Writing** Polish, self-assess or response partners assess using marking ladder (Resource Page K). Rework one identified area for improvement
	Flow Diagrams Plenary extends beyond Y2 framework by looping a flow diagram back on itself to make a cyclical diagram	*Writing Definitions*		

Labels and Captions

Objective

We will find out about headings, labels, captions and fonts and know the difference between labels and captions

You need: Resource Pages A–C and J; range of small non-fiction books with diagrams, illustrations, labels and captions; whiteboard or OHP.

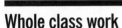

Whole class work

- Share-read Resource Page A. The children identify and annotate the main text. *How do we know this is the main text?* Answer: same font; same size; same verb tense; makes sense when read in order.

- *What would we call the other bits of text on these pages?* Answer: heading; labels; safety warning.

- The children come to the front to identify and highlight these features in different colours while you annotate their findings (see Resource Page B).

- *How do we know that these bits of text are different from the main text?* Answer: different font; size; use of bold or italic; not always in sentences; positioned separately from main text; clearly linked to diagrams or illustrations on the page; doesn't make sense if read straight through with main text.

- Read out the last line. *Is this a caption or main text?* The children justify their choice to response partner, then share with class.

- *What is the difference between a label and a caption?* Leave the children to think. The definition should emerge from independent work.

Independent, pair or guided work

- The children independently highlight and annotate *How food changes when it is cooked* (Resource Page A), identifying main text, labels and captions.

- *Can you explain the difference between labels and captions?* Answer: a label says what the picture/illustration shows; captions add extra information that isn't in the picture.

- More able children can go on to investigate the difference between a diagram and an illustration (Resource Page C).

Plenary

- Build a class checklist for labels, captions, diagrams and illustrations based on the children's findings (see Resource Page J for ideas). You may wish to break the checklist into several smaller ones, for example, one for diagrams, one for main text and so on.

Flow Diagrams

Objective

We will present information in a flow diagram

You need: Resource Pages D–F and J; whiteboard or OHP and OHT pens.

Whole class work

- Read the flow diagram (Resource Page E).

- Together, review the class checklist and revise the main features (Resource Page J).

- The children look at their notes from a science investigation. *Could we present this information in a flow diagram?*

- Demonstrate writing a flow chart. Use notes from a science investigation or examples of modelled writing (see Resource Page D).

- The children assess your flow chart using the checklist.

- Share-write the first step in the flow diagram of your science investigation.

Independent, pair or guided work

- The children continue the flow diagram independently, supported by writing frame (Resource Page F), using their own notes of the observation.

Plenary

- *What would the next step be after the last box in the flow diagram?* The children discuss with response partners, then share with the class.

- Show the children how the process can repeat itself indefinitely by creating a flow chart. Add curved arrows between boxes to make a circle and introduce the terms 'cycle' and 'cyclical'.

- Challenge the children to think of other data that would fit a cyclical diagram, for example, the seasons, life cycles, days of the week, rainfall, and so on.

- *Where would you begin reading a cyclical flow diagram?* Answer: at any point.

Writing Definitions

Objectives

We will use dictionaries and glossaries to locate words by using the initial letter. We will discuss what definitions are and explore some simple definitions in dictionaries

You need: Resource Pages G–I; dictionaries (class set if available); pair of scissors and Blu-tack™. This lesson assumes some knowledge of alphabetical texts.

Note

- The definitions that the children produce could be word-processed, likewise the glossary in the follow-up lesson.

Whole class work

- Read Resource Page G, *Heating Things*, and focus on the shaded words. Record these words as a class list on Resource Page H.

- *How could we find out what these words mean?* Explain that dictionaries can be used not only for checking spellings but to find out the definition of words. Ask a child to find the word 'definition' in a dictionary. While they are doing this, take the opportunity to review how to find a word in a dictionary:
  - *What letter does the word begin with?*
  - *Is that letter towards the beginning of the alphabet, the middle or the end?*
  - *Let's look at the top of the pages in the 'D' section to find words beginning with 'D' then 'E'.*
  - *Now use your finger to track down the words to find the definition.*

- Model writing a definition for the example 'solid': 'something which has a definite shape'. Record this on the class list. Explain that it is not necessary to write 'A solid is …', just the words that explain what the initial word means. Then ask a child to check your definition in the dictionary. Ask the children to give possible definitions for all the shaded words from the text. If a class set of dictionaries is available, the children could look up the words to check if their definitions were accurate.

- Once the class list is completed, separate the words from their definitions. Put the words into a pile and display the definitions on the board. Choose a child to select a word from the pile and ask another child to find the appropriate definition.

- Discuss the importance of having words organised alphabetically in dictionaries. Then ask the class to arrange the words from the list alphabetically. Show how to sort alphabetically when words begin with the same letter using the examples 'materials' and 'melt'.

Independent, pair or guided work

- Distribute Resource Page I, *Ice, Water and Steam*. Ask the children to read the text, then select three 'science' words which they think some children might find difficult to understand. The children write a definition for each, check it in a dictionary, and then write the words in alphabetical order.

Plenary

- Ask one or two children to read one of their definitions aloud. The rest of the class should refer to the text and try to decide which word has been chosen. Discuss the definitions.

(Pupil copymaster)

How food changes when it is cooked

All kinds of food can be cooked in an oven.

Lemon pudding

Cup cakes

Roast meat

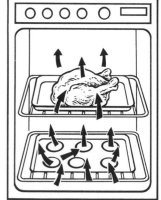

The heat is turned on to warm up the oven. Once the food is inside, the door is shut. The air inside the oven gets very hot.

The outside of the food gets hot first. Then the heat goes through the food and cooks it.

! TAKE CARE! When the door is opened, the heat rushes out.

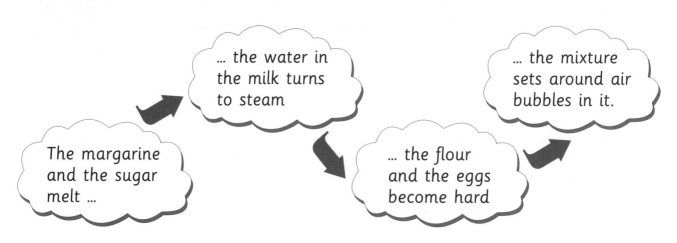

The margarine and the sugar melt ...

... the water in the milk turns to steam

... the flour and the eggs become hard

... the mixture sets around air bubbles in it.

based on What's Cooking, *by Christine Butterworth (Ginn All Aboard)*

Exemplar analysis

Example of analysis of *How food changes*

Heading.

Text in present tense.

Text.

Sentences use verbs in present tense.

Warning panel helps reader stay safe.

Bubbles contain text.

Ellipsis shows there is more information to come.

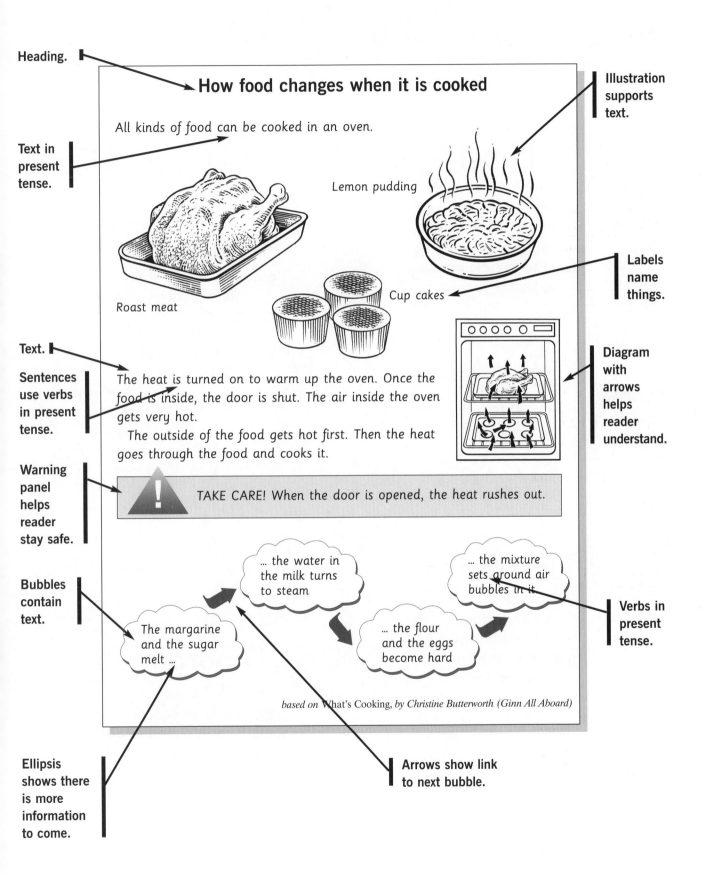

How food changes when it is cooked

All kinds of food can be cooked in an oven.

Lemon pudding

Cup cakes

Roast meat

The heat is turned on to warm up the oven. Once the food is inside, the door is shut. The air inside the oven gets very hot.

The outside of the food gets hot first. Then the heat goes through the food and cooks it.

TAKE CARE! When the door is opened, the heat rushes out.

... the water in the milk turns to steam

... the mixture sets around air bubbles in it

The margarine and the sugar melt ...

... the flour and the eggs become hard

based on What's Cooking, *by Christine Butterworth (Ginn All Aboard)*

Illustration supports text.

Labels name things.

Diagram with arrows helps reader understand.

Verbs in present tense.

Arrows show link to next bubble.

(Pupil copymaster)

Explanation terms

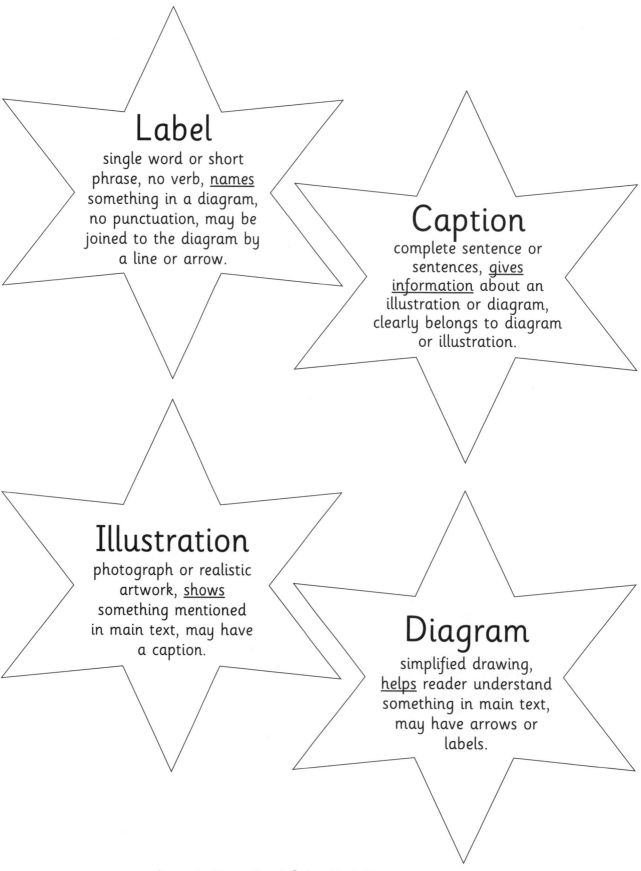

Label
single word or short phrase, no verb, <u>names</u> something in a diagram, no punctuation, may be joined to the diagram by a line or arrow.

Caption
complete sentence or sentences, <u>gives information</u> about an illustration or diagram, clearly belongs to diagram or illustration.

Illustration
photograph or realistic artwork, <u>shows</u> something mentioned in main text, may have a caption.

Diagram
simplified drawing, <u>helps</u> reader understand something in main text, may have arrows or labels.

(Exemplar material)

Modelled writing

How do you get an ice cube out of a glass of water without getting wet?

You will need ...
a glass
water
ice cube
salt
piece of string

1. Sprinkle some salt on the ice.
2. Pick up the string and dangle one end on top of the ice cube and leave for 3 minutes.
3. Pick up the string to lift the ice cube out of the glass.

What's happening?

Salt melts the ice a little bit, so the string is soaked in water. But there's not enough salt to melt the whole cube. When the ice re-freezes the string is trapped in the new ice.

This is why the sea doesn't freeze even when large lakes freeze over. The salt in the water means it has to be very cold for the ice to form – then we get icebergs.

This is why people put salt on icy roads in the winter.

Pupil copymaster

Flow diagram

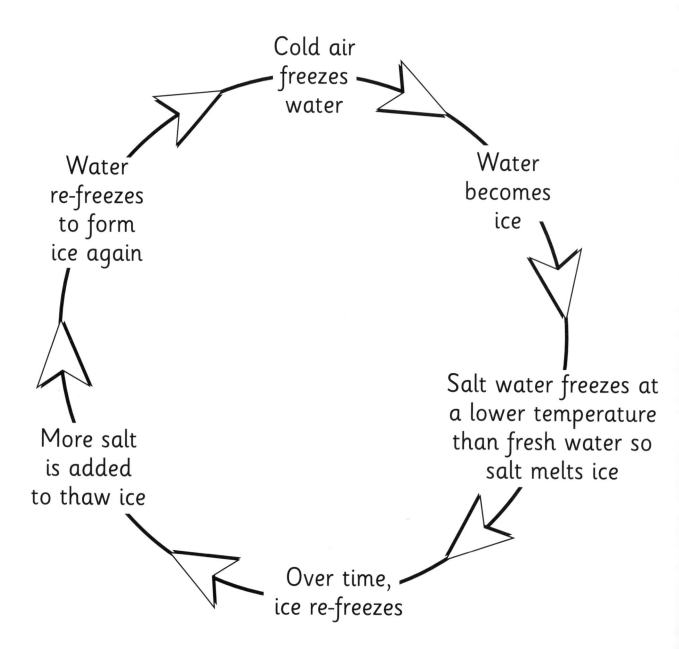

(**Pupil copymaster**)

Writing frame

Heading – what you want to find out

_____

Main text

_____

_____

_____

_____

_____

_____

Safety notice

_____

What's happening? (Explanation)

_____

_____

_____

_____

(**Pupil copymaster**)

Heating things

Some solid things go runny and turn into a liquid when you heat them. We call this melting.

Ice melts into water

When ice is warmed it melts – it turns into water.

Heating other solid materials

The more you heat something, the quicker it melts.

Chocolate will melt slowly if you leave it in the sunshine.
If you heat it in a saucepan, it will melt very quickly.

based on CGP's KS1 Science Study Book

Classworks Literacy Year 2 © Sara Moult, Nelson Thornes Ltd 2003

(Pupil copymaster)

Class glossary

Word	Definition

Pupil copymaster

Ice, Water and Steam

Turning water into steam

If you heat water enough it will boil.
When it boils it turns into steam.

Steam can be very DANGEROUS. It
can burn you badly.

Old-fashioned trains used steam
to push them along.

Ice, water and steam

Remember – ice, water and steam are all the SAME MATERIAL.
Ice and steam are just different forms of water.

based on CGP's KS1 Science Study Book

(**Exemplar material**)

Checklist for explanation texts

- Use a heading in a large, clear font

- Heading should state nature of investigation or ask a question that investigation will try to solve

- Make sure main text is clear and written in the order that things happen

- Use the present tense

- Use illustrations or pictures to give the reader more information

- Use diagrams to explain something to the reader

- Label illustrations, pictures and diagrams

- Use captions to give more information about what is happening in the picture

- Use arrows to direct the reader to the next thing that happens

- Highlight safety notices in a box

- Use a sub-heading to introduce extra information

- Begin sentences with a capital letter and end them with a full stop

- End safety notices with an exclamation mark

Classworks Literacy Year 2 © Sara Moult, Nelson Thornes Ltd 2003

Marking ladder

Name: _____

Pupil	Objective	Teacher
	I used a heading in a large, clear font.	
	My main text is written in the order that things happen.	
	I used illustrations and diagrams with labels and captions.	
	I used arrows to show the order things happen.	
	I used a safety notice in a box with an exclamation mark.	
	I used sentences beginning with a capital letter and ending with a full stop.	
	I used the present tense.	
	What could I do to improve my explanation next time?	

Information Texts

Outcome

An information text using questions as headings, with front cover, blurb, sub-headings, captions, labelled diagrams, contents page, introduction and conclusion, in the form of a concertina book

Objectives

Sentence

6 to turn statements into questions, learning a range of 'wh' words typically used to open questions: 'what', 'where', 'when', 'who' and to add question marks.

Text

13 to understand the distinction between fact and fiction; to use terms 'fact', 'fiction' and 'non-fiction' appropriately.

14 to pose questions and record these in writing, prior to reading non-fiction to find answers.

15 to use a contents page to find way about text.

16 to scan a text to find specific sections, e.g. key words or phrases, sub-headings.

17 to skim-read title, contents page, illustrations, chapter headings and sub-headings, to speculate what a book might be about.

20 to write non-fiction texts, using texts read as models for own writing, e.g. use of headings, sub-headings, captions.

Planning frame

- Read and analyse contents and title pages of information texts.

- Identify key features of introduction.

- Write own introduction.

- Repeat for information pages, cover and blurb.

- Assemble and edit completed booklet.

Notes

- This longer unit has cross-curricular links with Science, especially QCA Unit 2b, 'Plants and Animals in the Local Environment', though it can be adapted to link to other units.

- The children could use the shared text as a model for writing about creatures such as minibeasts that they have observed and investigated in science lessons.

- Tackle this non-fiction text by dipping in and out using the contents page as a guide rather than reading it from beginning to end.

How you could plan this unit

Day 1	Day 2	Day 3	Day 4	Day 5
Reading and analysis Skim-read cover and contents page of information book to identify text type. Begin checklist of features of main text. Leave page 1 of concertina books blank to complete as cover page at end of unit	**Reading and analysis** Read and annotate introduction from an information book using checklist. Identify key features of introduction (see Resource Page I)	**Writing** *The Introduction* Page 3 of concertina books	**Reading and analysis** Read the contents pages of several information books and identify that a contents page gives a useful summary of main topics. On whiteboards, compose a list of main topics from the shared text (Resource Page B)	**Writing** Model writing a content planning sheet for book on minibeasts. The children plan and list main topics to cover in their own books, acting as a draft contents page (Resource Page D). This will eventually form page 2 of concertina books

Day 6	Day 7	Day 8	Day 9	Day 10
Reading and analysis Select a section from the contents page of an information book on minibeasts. Read and annotate using checklist from Day 1	**Writing** Model writing on chosen minibeast, using example from Day 6. The children write their own first information page, following the format but using their planned topic. This forms page 4 of concertina books	**Reading and analysis** *Questions and Answers*	**Writing** Model writing a further page, developing the use of questions and answers from Day 8. The children write their own text for page 5 of their books, answering the questions identified (Resource Page F)	**Reading and analysis** Select another section from contents page. Read and annotate using checklist from Day 1

Day 11	Day 12	Day 13	Day 14	Day 15
Writing Model writing. The children continue with shared/ supported writing to form page 6 of their concertina books	**Reading and analysis** Analyse covers, title and blurb and annotate. Use the blurb from a class text to discuss the form and function of mini-summary of information on back cover. Use non-fiction books from school library. Discuss factual style of titles	**Writing** *Writing the Cover and Blurb* Pages 1 and 8 of concertina books	**Analysis** Produce master checklist and marking ladder for information book on minibeasts. Guide groups as appropriate in compiling an index/glossary using key words identified on planning sheet. This forms page 7 of concertina books	**Evaluation** Complete, assemble and assess work against marking ladder. Edit and rework where necessary. The children can write up their planned contents page as a final draft

Concertina book summary

1. Front cover	2. Contents page	3. Introduction	4. Text 1
5. Text 2	6. Text 3	7. Index/glossary	8. Back cover

The Introduction

Objectives

We will write an introduction to an information booklet about minibeasts. We will write in clear sentences using capital letters and full stops correctly

You need: Resource Pages A, B and I; class observations/notes of creatures from science investigation; class work on minibeasts; coloured pencils; flip chart and coloured pens; A4 whiteboards and pens.

Whole class work

- Model writing an introduction (Resource Page A). Use rainbow sentences to help the children see sentence demarcation clearly, and refer to the class checklist as you work (see Resource Page I for ideas).

- The children assess your text against the checklist, first with a response partner, then together as a class (*Think, Pair, Share*).

- Discuss how the introduction could be made livelier, for example, with the use of more powerful verbs and interesting adjectives.

- With your class, share-write using a question as a heading and the second example as a model.

Independent, pair or guided work

- In pairs, the children ring or highlight each separate sentence of the introduction on Resource Page B in a different colour.

- The children then discuss these findings with another pair (*Walk to Talk*).

- Take feedback and ask:
  - *How many sentences are there?*
  - *What do you notice about the beginnings?*
  - *Which one is repeated and why?*
  - *What do you notice about the verbs?*

Plenary

- The children attempt their own introduction using the checklist and one or both of the shared texts as a model.

- Challenge your guided group to 'hook' the reader by using direct questions in the text.

- Evaluate using a response sandwich: one good comment; one area for improvement; another good comment.

Questions and Answers

Objectives

We will ask questions before reading, then find the answer in our text. We will also turn statements into questions, using 'wh' words

You need: Resource Pages B (class set), C, E and I; A4 whiteboards and pens; whiteboard or acetate overlay and OHT pens; *Looking After the Egg*, by Meredith Hooper, or other information book about penguins.

Whole class work

- Explain that today the class will be reading some more about penguins. In pairs, the children plan a series of questions to focus their reading, based on some or all of the question words on Resource Page E.

- Record a selection of their questions and display them during the shared read.

- Read Resource Page B, discuss and annotate (see Resource Page C).

- Add annotations to the class checklist (see Resource Page I for ideas).

Independent, pair or guided work

- In pairs, the children annotate their copies of Resource Page B, listing any extra features for the class checklist.

- Your guided group can annotate a text with additional features, for example, fact boxes, flow charts or a life cycle diagram.

- *What questions did we ask and did we find the answers?*

- Formulate questions for the next lesson. *What do we want to find out?*

Plenary

- The drama activity 'Penguin Shuffle' provides a opportunity to encourage group co-operation. The children stand in a clear space, feet together, hands tightly by sides, visualising a precious, fragile penguin egg on their feet. Using slow, tiny, shuffling steps, they move in together as closely as possible, those on the outside facing inwards. They will be amazed at how quickly the heat builds up.

- On the word 'Blizzard!' those on the outside begin slowly and gently to shuffle their way to the centre and those in the centre work their way outwards, while keeping the huddle really tight.

- Describe the fierce, bitterly cold blizzard as the children huddle.

- Stop when everyone has had a turn inside and on the edge of the huddle.
  - *What do you think would happen if the penguins in the middle wouldn't take turns on the outside?*
  - *How do you think penguins learned to behave like this?*
  - *How did it feel to be in the middle/on the outside?*
  - *Would you like to be a penguin? Why/why not?*
  - *What have you learned from this activity?*

Writing the Cover and Blurb

Objectives

We will write a cover page and a blurb for our information book

You need: Resource Pages G and H; whiteboards and pens; large piece of sugar paper; a range of non-fiction texts for reference; fiction and non-fiction texts for the plenary.

Whole class work

- Refer back to the previous lesson's analysis of the front and back covers of non-fiction information books.

- In pairs, tell your partner three things that you might find on the front of a book (title, author, illustrator, publisher, series …) and three things that you might find on the back cover (blurb, other titles in series, publisher, ISBN panel, price …).

- Make a shared list of suggestions, then check against a sample text to make sure that nothing has been left out. This will act as a class checklist for independent work.

- Model how they are going to arrange this information by writing your own title, author, publisher, blurb and ISBN panel on a large piece of sugar paper, folded in half to represent the front and back covers.

- Using whiteboards, the children plan their front cover on one side and their back cover on the reverse.

- Read through a couple of the planning boards as a class, highlighting effective composition and addressing any mistakes.

Independent, pair or guided work

- The children take their planning boards back to their tables and in independent or guided groups work on designing their front and back covers.

- Encourage them to refer to the shared checklist to check their work, and have examples of non-fiction information books readily available for inspiration.

Plenary

- 'Name that Blurb' challenge: give each child a response card, copied from Resource Pages G and H so that each card as 'fiction' on one side and 'non-fiction' on the reverse. Read out examples of blurbs from a range of fiction and non-fiction books chosen from your class collection. Pause after each one for the children to vote with response cards whether they think it is a fiction or a non-fiction text.

- Recap on the purpose and organisation of cover information to inform and 'hook' the reader.

(Exemplar material)

Modelled writing

Introduction

Ants are tiny members of the insect family. They are very common and can be found in most parts of the world. Ants live together in big groups.

An ant's body is in three parts. Six legs all grow from the middle part.

Ants like to live underground where it is dark and cool. They choose dry sandy places to build their nests.

A livelier version

What are ants?

Have you ever been bitten by ants, perhaps on a picnic or in the garden? Did you know that they are insects? These tiny creatures are found almost everywhere in the world.

(Pupil copymaster)

Looking After the Egg

Introduction

Emperor penguins are the largest penguins in the world. They are about as tall as a seven-year-old child. But they are much heavier.

Emperor penguins are 1.15 metres tall. They weigh 40 kilograms.

Emperor penguins live in the coldest, windiest place on Earth. They live in the **Antarctic**.

Winter eggs

Emperor penguins lay their eggs in winter. All the other penguins living in the Antarctic lay their eggs in spring.

| Adélie | Gentoo | Chinstrap |
| Macaroni | King | Emperor |

Six species of penguin lay their eggs and bring up their chicks in the Antarctic.

Winter in the Antarctic is extremely cold. Freezing winds blow across the ice. In the middle of winter, it is dark all day as well as all night.

Keeping warm

The male Emperor penguins stand on the ice looking after the eggs. They stand day after day, week after week. It is dark. In the middle of winter the sun never rises. The only light comes from the moon, and the stars.

When cold winds blow the penguins stand very still. They hunch their heads down into their shoulders to keep warm.

They have a thick layer of fat under their skin. It helps protect them from the cold. Their feathers are waterproof and windproof to keep out the cold.

Emperor penguins have four layers of feathers to protect them from cold.

down   skin

feathers

Hooks hold the feathers firmly in the skin.

Based on Looking After the Egg, *by Meredith Hooper*

Classworks Literacy Year 2 © Sara Moult, Nelson Thornes Ltd 2003

(Exemplar analysis)

Example of analysis of *Looking After the Egg*

Heading.

Bold shows word is in the glossary.

Introduction opens with topic.

Present tense.

General facts.

Label – names penguin in the illustration.

Font changes to show that captions are different from the main text.

Caption gives more information about the pictures.

Sub-heading.

Caption.

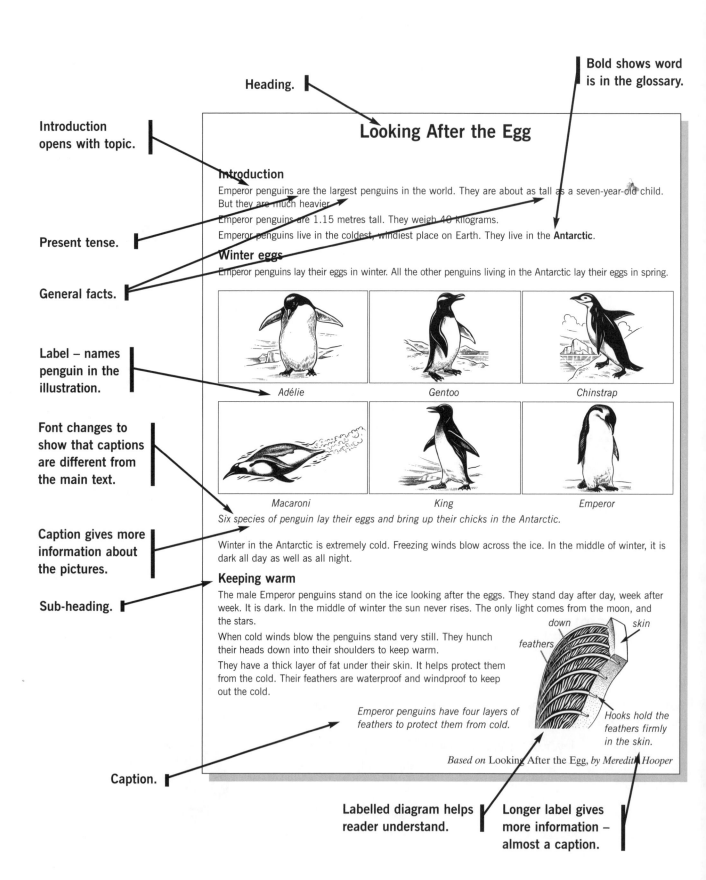

Looking After the Egg

Introduction

Emperor penguins are the largest penguins in the world. They are about as tall as a seven-year-old child. But they are much heavier.
Emperor penguins are 1.15 metres tall. They weigh 40 kilograms.
Emperor penguins live in the coldest, windiest place on Earth. They live in the **Antarctic**.

Winter eggs

Emperor penguins lay their eggs in winter. All the other penguins living in the Antarctic lay their eggs in spring.

Adélie

Gentoo

Chinstrap

Macaroni

King

Emperor

Six species of penguin lay their eggs and bring up their chicks in the Antarctic.

Winter in the Antarctic is extremely cold. Freezing winds blow across the ice. In the middle of winter, it is dark all day as well as all night.

Keeping warm

The male Emperor penguins stand on the ice looking after the eggs. They stand day after day, week after week. It is dark. In the middle of winter the sun never rises. The only light comes from the moon, and the stars.

When cold winds blow the penguins stand very still. They hunch their heads down into their shoulders to keep warm.

They have a thick layer of fat under their skin. It helps protect them from the cold. Their feathers are waterproof and windproof to keep out the cold.

Emperor penguins have four layers of feathers to protect them from cold.

down   skin

feathers

Hooks hold the feathers firmly in the skin.

Based on Looking After the Egg, *by Meredith Hooper*

Labelled diagram helps reader understand.

Longer label gives more information – almost a caption.

Classworks Literacy Year 2 © Sara Moult, Nelson Thornes Ltd 2003

(**Pupil copymaster**)

Content planner

Name _____

My information book is about _____

_____

Topic for page	Planning notes
Key words	

Pupil copymaster

Question words

What ?

Where ?

When ?

Who ?

How ?

(Pupil copymaster)

Writing frame

What are woodlice?

Have you ever watched a woodlouse _____

_____ ?

Have you wondered how it _____

and why it _____

_____ ?

Woodlice are tiny creatures with _____ legs.

They like to live _____

_____

_____

_____ .

(Pupil copymaster)

Response cards (side A)

fiction	*fiction*
fiction	*fiction*
fiction	*fiction*
fiction	*fiction*
fiction	*fiction*
fiction	*fiction*
fiction	*fiction*
fiction	*fiction*
fiction	*fiction*
fiction	*fiction*
fiction	*fiction*
fiction	*fiction*

Pupil copymaster

Response cards (side B)

non-fiction	non-fiction
non-fiction	non-fiction
non-fiction	non-fiction
non-fiction	non-fiction
non-fiction	non-fiction
non-fiction	non-fiction
non-fiction	non-fiction
non-fiction	non-fiction
non-fiction	non-fiction
non-fiction	non-fiction
non-fiction	non-fiction
non-fiction	non-fiction

(Exemplar material)

Checklist for the introduction of an information text

- Use the heading 'Introduction'

- Write in the present tense

- First sentence gives the topic and an important fact

- Add two or three more sentences giving general facts

- Final sentence repeats topic and gives another fact

- Draw a clear, simple picture of the topic

- Write a caption giving two more facts in two short sentences

(**Marking ladder**)

Name: _____

Pupil	Objective	Teacher
	My front cover and title give clues to contents.	
	I included a contents page to guide reader.	
	I used headings and sub-headings to organise information.	
	I used questions as headings to engage the reader.	
	I used the present tense.	
	I used captions to give more information about illustrations.	
	I used labelled diagrams to help the reader.	
	I included an introduction and a conclusion directly addressed to the reader.	
	I included a blurb on the back cover to hook the reader.	
	What could I do to improve my information text next time?	

Alphabetically Ordered Texts

Outcome

A glossary and index linked to a current area of study

Objectives

Text

16 to use dictionaries and glossaries to locate words by using initial letter.

17 [be taught] that dictionaries and glossaries give definitions and explanations; discuss what definitions are, explore some simple definitions in dictionaries.

18 to use other alphabetically ordered texts, e.g. indexes, directories, listings, registers; to discuss how they are used.

20 to make class dictionaries and glossaries of special interest words, giving explanations and definitions, e.g. linked to topics.

Planning frame

- Compile an alphabetical list of topic words and phrases complete with definitions.

Note

- This unit lends itself to cross-curricular links, particularly to Science, History or Geography QCA units, for example, Primary History Unit 5, 'How do we know about the Great Fire of London?' Any unit with a bank of words specific to a subject could be linked, but it is important to have a meaningful and current word bank.

Extension activity

- To help the children put their learning in context and to extend their understanding of different cultures and conventions, why not show them an example of some text – a book or newspaper page – in Chinese? Demonstrate how the text can run in lines or columns, how the book opens 'back to front'. Explain that there is no Chinese alphabet. All the characters have to be learned and recognised on sight. Simple characters are combined and grouped to produce new characters. An average vocabulary requires recognition of 4000 different characters.

- Ask the children how a Chinese dictionary might be organised. Answer: It's very difficult! Characters are made up of a 'phonetic' part (indicating how it should be pronounced) and the part that is listed in stroke order, the 'radical'. So first you would have to look up the radical and then count the number of strokes in the other half of the character. It is quite complicated and means that you have to know how to write the characters correctly or you may get the number of strokes wrong. Chinese children are still learning to write in Year 6 because there are so many characters to learn.

How you could plan this unit

Day 1	Day 2	Day 3	Day 4	Day 5
Reading and analysis	Reading, writing and analysis Annotate dictionary and glossary using checklist (see Resource Page H for ideas)	Writing	Reading and analysis Analyse index and annotate using checklist (see Resource Page H for ideas)	Writing
Using a Dictionary		*Writing a Glossary*		*Writing an Index*

Using a Dictionary

Objective

We will see how a dictionary works and use one to find words we want

You need: Resource Pages A, B, E and H; sample pages from children's dictionary; class set of dictionaries; whiteboard, OHT or flip chart; alphabetically sequenced CD-ROM reference tool linked to cross-curricular unit, for example encyclopaedia; large alphabet strip on display; word bank from recent work.

Whole class work

- Ask the children to bring in examples of alphabetically ordered texts for display. Add something unusual, for example, a set of inserts for a ring binder.

- Ask the children to vote how confident they feel about being able to quickly find words in a dictionary. Thumbs up = confident; thumbs down = I need help; thumb horizontal = I'm beginning to understand.

- Warm up with a familiar alphabet rap or song.

- Introduce Resource Pages A and B. Identify text type and purpose. Introduce the term 'definition'.

- Remind the children, *We never start a dictionary search by opening at random or turning pages from the beginning.* Demonstrate 'quick access' to the dictionary (Resource Page E).

- *Why don't our markers look evenly spaced on the alphabet strip?* Answer: because some letters are more common at the beginnings of words than others, for example, lots more words start with 'a', 'p' or 'c' than with 'j', 'q' or 'y'.

- In pairs, the children take turns to hold the dictionary. *Who will be first to find these sections – 'p', 't', 'h', 'b', 'o', 'k'?*

- Explain that quick access gets more important as the alphabetical texts they want to use get thicker. Show the children an encyclopaedia, a phone directory or another reference book from the display to illustrate.

- *How long would it take to find a word starting with 'y' in this book if you turned pages one at a time? How is this different from the way we read a fiction book?*

Independent, pair or guided work

- Have a bank of five to ten familiar words from a recent topic, ensuring that no two words start with the same letter. Jumble them up so they are not in alphabetical order. In pairs, taking turns with the dictionary and working collaboratively, the children see how quickly they can find the words and read their definitions.

- Have a second, shorter list (with the same initial letter) ready to challenge faster workers. *Can you work out any rules for when words start with the same letter?*

- ICT: same task using CD-ROM dictionary.

Plenary

- *How confident do you feel about finding a word in the dictionary now? Show me with your thumb.*

- Together, put together a class checklist for using a dictionary (Resource Page H).

Writing a Glossary

Objective

We will write a class glossary for an information book about ... [a current topic]

You need: Resource Page H; big book with a glossary; sample dictionary pages; word bank from recent unit or work; A4 whiteboards and pens.

Whole class work

- *What is the difference between a dictionary and a glossary?* Think, pair, share.

- Take feedback and list differences on board (see Resource Page H for ideas).

- *How would you define a glossary?* Share-write the answer:

> A glossary is a short, simple list of definitions for specific words and technical terms from a single book on a single topic – usually found at the end of a non-fiction book.

- Model writing a definition for one of the words or terms in the topic bank:

> thatch   straw or reeds laid out and pinned down to make the roof of a house or other building.
>
> thatched, thatcher

- Share-write a second definition from your class list.

- In pairs, the children tackle a third word or term on their whiteboards.

Independent, pair or guided work

- The children write definitions for the rest of the words and terms in the bank.

- By the time these glossaries are being written, the children should be thoroughly familiar with the terms on the list. If necessary, they can find them in a dictionary in advance of this lesson. The independent session is intended for the children to write their own definitions without using dictionaries. If dictionaries are available, they will be tempted to copy without necessarily understanding what they write. Allow them to consult each other and orally rehearse definitions ahead of writing.

- Some children may have time to finish their definition by adding a sentence to put the word or term in context. Demonstrate that not just any sentence will do:

> A spark set the <u>thatch</u> on the house roof on fire.
> [gives clue about properties of thatch]
>
> The house roof was made of <u>thatch</u>.
> [no clue to properties of thatch]

Plenary

- Share some definitions and pool ideas.

- Share-write a final class version for all words and terms.

- Trail the next lesson (Day 4) by showing an index page from the big book. *What do you think it is for?*

Writing an Index

Objective

We will write an index for a class book

You need: a class text related to a current topic; Resource Page F or relevant word
bank, copied on to card and cut up (one set per group and one for
teacher); Resource Page G (one per group, enlarged to A3); Blu-tack™.

Note

- The written outcome of this unit needs to reflect a cross-curricular link, for example QCA History Unit 5, 'How do we know about the Great Fire of London?' Choose a relevant non-fiction information text from your classroom collection, preferably a 'big book', and Blu-tack™ a blank sheet of paper over the index page.

Whole class work

- Read with your class the title of the text you have chosen. Ask the children in pairs to decide what type of book they think it is going to be. Recap on the clues the cover offers, e.g. factual title, photo or 'old-style' drawing, series name, classification.

- Without opening the book, explain to the children that they don't have the time to read the whole book through but that they need to find quickly an important piece of information. For example, **We know that the Great Fire of London is said to have started in Pudding Lane, but we don't know where Pudding Lane is.**

- Challenge them to tell you where you should start looking, referring back to the reading and analysis from Day 4 and deciding that the best place to look is the index.

- Ask a child to come up and turn to the index for you – they will find that it has disappeared! This will provide the purpose for the day's writing challenge: to make a new index so that we can use the book again.

- **How are we going to write an index?** Challenge the children to remember the points identified on your index checklist from Day 4.

- Use the key word cards (Resource Page F) or your own key words and demonstrate composing an index by putting them into alphabetical order with Blu-tack™ on the blank index frame (Resource Page G).

- When the class has checked the order, skim-read the book with the class, looking for the key words. Write the corresponding page numbers next to the words. Model separating two or more numbers for the same key word with a comma.

Independent, pair or guided work

- Give each group a blank frame and a set of key words to order alphabetically. Tailor the challenge to suit each group by varying the number/complexity of key words.

- Encourage discussion in this activity: the group needs to agree on the order of key words and rearrange as necessary before sticking on to the frame in order.

Plenary

- (Groups will need to stay in groups for this plenary.) Read the text aloud to your class, pointing out the new page number as you turn each page. The children listen carefully and jot down page numbers next to their key words as they hear them.

- Remind them to separate a string of numbers for the same key word with commas.

- Reinforce the use of index in guided reading sessions this week.

(Pupil copymaster)

An illustrated dictionary – left-hand page

sleep

sleep sleeps sleeping slept *verb*
When you sleep, you close your eyes and rest your body as you do in bed at night. *I slept for eight hours last night.*
sleep *noun.*

sleepy sleepier sleepiest *adjective*
When you are sleepy, you feel tired and it is hard to keep your eyes open.

sleeve sleeves *noun*
the part of a shirt, a coat or a dress that covers your arm.

sleigh sleighs *noun*
a vehicle that you sit on to move over snow. Sleighs are usually pulled by animals such as horses or reindeer.
▲ Say *slay*.

slice slices *noun*
a thin, flat piece that has been cut from something. *A slice of cake.*

slide slides sliding slid *verb*
When something slides, it moves smoothly over a surface. *The children were sliding on the ice.*

slide slides *noun*
something that you play on. You climb up the steps on one side and slide down the other side.

slight *adjective*
small or not very important. *I've got a slight earache.*
slightly *adverb.*

slimy slimier slimiest *adjective*
dirty and slippery. *The rocks were covered with slimy seaweed.*

slow slower slowest *adjective*
Somebody or something that is slow does not move quickly. *Snails and tortoises are very slow animals.* ■ The opposite is **fast**.
slowly *adverb*
We walked home slowly.

slug slugs *noun*
a small slimy animal like a snail without a shell. Gardeners do not like slugs because they eat plants.

sly slyer slyest *adjective*
If somebody is sly, they are clever in a secret and not very nice way. *That was a very sly trick.*

small smaller smallest *adjective*
not very big. *Ants are small insects.* ◆ *My brother is smaller than me.*
■ The opposite is **big** or **large**.

---

small

Some words you can use instead of small:

All small animals look sweet.
☞ **baby, young**

The writing is so small you need a magnifying glass to read it.
☞ **minute, tiny**

Don't worry. It's only a small mistake.
☞ **unimportant, slight, minor**

Centipedes have lots of small legs.
☞ **short**

---

smart smarter smartest *adjective*
1 neat and tidy. *Dad wears a smart suit for work.*
2 clever. *You're too smart for this quiz!*

smash smashes smashing smashed *verb*
If something smashes, it breaks into a lot of pieces. *I dropped the plate and it smashed on the floor.*

smell smells smelling smelt or smelled *verb*
1 When you smell something, you use your nose to find out about it. *I can smell food cooking in the kitchen.*
2 When something smells, you notice it with your nose. *She smells of soap.*
smelly *adjective. Smelly old socks.*

smile smiles smiling smiled *verb*
When you smile, the corners of your mouth turn up to show that you are happy.
smile *noun*

smoke smokes smoking smoked *verb*
When somebody smokes, they have a cigarette or a pipe in their mouth, and breathe the smoke in and out

smoke smokes *noun*
the white, grey or black stuff that you see going up in the air when something is burning. *Smoke was pouring out of the chimney.*

smooth smoother smoothest *adjective*
If something is smooth, you cannot feel lumps or any rough parts when you touch it. *These vases have smooth surfaces.*
smoothly *adverb.*

(Pupil copymaster)

An illustrated dictionary – right-hand page

solid

snack snacks *noun*
a small amount of food that you eat when you are in a hurry. *We had a quick snack of cheese on toast.*

snail snails *noun*
a small creature with a hard shell on its back. Snails move along very slowly.

snap snaps snapping snapped *verb*
1 When something snaps, it breaks and makes a sudden sharp sound. *The pencil snapped when I stepped on it.*
2 When a dog snaps, it tries to bite somebody or something. *The dog snapped at us when we walked by.*
3 When a person snaps, they speak in an angry way. *"Be quiet," she snapped.*

snatch snatches snatching snatched *verb*
If you snatch something, you take it quickly and roughly. *The thief snatched her purse.*

snore snores snoring snored *verb*
When somebody snores, they breathe noisily when they are asleep.

snout snouts *noun*
the nose and mouth of an animal such as a pig or a badger.

snow *noun*
small, white piece of frozen water that falls from the sky when it is very cold.
snow *verb*, **snowy** *adjective*.

snowboarding *noun*
a sport where you move down snowy hills on a piece of wood or metal that looks like a skateboard without wheels.

snowflake snowflakes *noun*
a small piece of falling snow. Snowflakes are star-shaped ice crystals.

soak soaks soaking soaked *verb*
1 When you soak something, you put it in water and leave it for a long time.
2 If you get soaked, you get very wet. *We got soaked in the rain.*

sob sobs sobbing sobbed *verb*
When you sob, you cry loudly.

soccer *noun*
a game of football, played by two teams of eleven players. The teams try to score goals by kicking a ball into a net at each end of a field called a pitch.

society societies *noun*
1 all the people who live in the same country or area and have the same laws and customs.
2 a kind of club for people who like the same things. *A drama society.*

socket sockets *noun*
a thing in a wall with holes where you can push in an electric plug.

sofa sofas *noun*
a long, comfortable seat for two or more people, also called a settee.

soft softer softest *adjective*
1 not hard or rough. *Cats have soft fur.*
2 not firm or stiff. *Soft snow.*
3 not loud, quiet and gentle. *He has a soft voice.*
4 too kind. *The teacher is too soft, so her class is always noisy.*
softly *adverb*, **soften** *verb*
The butter is very hard because it has been in the refrigerator. We should leave it out to soften.

software *noun*
the part inside a computer or on a computer disk that has the instructions that make a computer work.

soil *noun*
the brown stuff, also called earth, that plants grow in.

solar *adjective*
to do with the Sun. *The Solar System.*

soldier soldiers *noun*
a person in an army. ▲ Say *sole-jer*

solid solids *noun*
an object that is hard and not a liquid or a gas. *Water is a liquid but ice is a solid.*

(Exemplar analysis)

Example of analysis of *An illustrated dictionary*

Guide words – show first and last words on double page – allows reader to check if desired word is between them.

Key word in bold.

Opposites shown where appropriate.

Verb tense changes shown.

Thesaurus box.

Example sentence in italics uses key word in context.

An illustrated dictionary – left-hand page

sleep

sleep sleeps sleeping slept *verb*
When you sleep, you close your eyes and rest your body as you do in bed at night. *I slept for eight hours last night.*
sleep *noun.*

sleepy sleepier sleepiest *adjective*
When you are sleepy, you feel tired and it is hard to keep your eyes open.

sleeve sleeves *noun*
the part of a shirt, a coat or a dress that covers your arm.

sleigh sleighs *noun*
a vehicle that you sit on to move over snow. Sleighs are usually pulled by animals such as horses or reindeer.
▲ Say *slay*.

slice slices *noun*
a thin, flat piece that has been cut from something. *A slice of cake.*

slide slides sliding slid *verb*
When something slides, it moves smoothly over a surface. *The children were sliding on the ice.*

slide slides *noun*
something that you play on. You climb up the steps on one side and slide down the other side.

slight *adjective*
small or not very important. *I've got a slight earache.*
slightly *adverb.*

slimy slimier slimiest *adjective*
dirty and slippery. *The rocks were covered with slimy seaweed.*

slow slower slowest *adjective*
Somebody or something that is slow does not move quickly. *Snails and tortoises are very slow animals.* ■ The opposite is **fast**.
slowly *adverb*
We walked home slowly.

slug slugs *noun*
a small slimy animal like a snail without a shell. Gardeners do not like slugs because they eat plants.

sly slyer slyest *adjective*
If somebody is sly, they are clever in a secret and not very nice way. *That was a very sly trick.*

small smaller smallest *adjective*
not very big. *Ants are small insects.* ◆ My brother is smaller than me.
■ The opposite is **big** or **large**.

---
small

Some words you can use instead of small:

All small animals look sweet.
☞ ***baby, young***

The writing is so small you need a magnifying glass to read it.
☞ ***minute, tiny***

Don't worry. It's only a small mistake.
☞ ***unimportant, slight, minor***

Centipedes have lots of small legs.
☞ ***short***

---

smart smarter smartest *adjective*
1 neat and tidy. *Dad wears a smart suit for work.*
2 clever. *You're too smart for this quiz!*

smash smashes smashing smashed *verb*
If something smashes, it breaks into a lot of pieces. *I dropped the plate and it smashed on the floor.*

smell smells smelling smelt or smelled *verb*
1 When you smell something, you use your nose to find out about it. *I can smell food cooking in the kitchen.*
2 When something smells, you notice it with your nose. *She smells of soap.*
smelly *adjective. Smelly old socks.*

smile smiles smiling smiled *verb*
When you smile, the corners of your mouth turn up to show that you are happy.
smile *noun*

smoke smokes smoking smoked *verb*
When somebody smokes, they have a cigarette or a pipe in their mouth, and breathe the smoke in and out

smoke smokes *noun*
the white, grey or black stuff that you see going up in the air when something is burning. *Smoke was pouring out of the chimney.*

smooth smoother smoothest *adjective*
If something is smooth, you cannot feel lumps or any rough parts when you touch it. *These vases have smooth surfaces.*
smoothly *adverb.*

Exemplar analysis

Example of analysis of *An illustrated dictionary (cont.)*

An illustrated dictionary – right-hand page

Definition avoids key word and is not a sentence.

Variations on word shown.

Multiple meanings numbered.

solid

snack snacks *noun*
a small amount of food that you eat when you are in a hurry. *We had a quick snack of cheese on toast.*

snail snails *noun*
a small creature with a hard shell on its back. Snails move along very slowly.

snap snaps snapping snapped *verb*
1 When something snaps, it breaks and makes a sudden sharp sound. *The pencil snapped when I stepped on it.*
2 When a dog snaps, it tries to bite somebody or something. *The dog snapped at us when we walked by.*
3 When a person snaps, they speak in an angry way. *"Be quiet," she snapped.*

snatch snatches snatching snatched *verb*
If you snatch something, you take it quickly and roughly. *The thief snatched her purse.*

snore snores snoring snored *verb*
When somebody snores, they breathe noisily when they are asleep.

snout snouts *noun*
the nose and mouth of an animal such as a pig or a badger.

snow *noun*
small, white piece of frozen water that falls from the sky when it is very cold.
snow *verb*, **snowy** *adjective*.

snowboarding *noun*
a sport where you move down snowy hills on a piece of wood or metal that looks like a skateboard without wheels.

snowflake snowflakes *noun*
a small piece of falling snow. Snowflakes are star-shaped ice crystals.

soak soaks soaking soaked *verb*
1 When you soak something, you put it in water and leave it for a long time.
2 If you get soaked, you get very wet. *We got soaked in the rain.*

sob sobs sobbing sobbed *verb*
When you sob, you cry loudly.

soccer *noun*
a game of football, played by two teams of eleven players. The teams try to score goals by kicking a ball into a net at each end of a field called a pitch.

society societies *noun*
1 all the people who live in the same country or area and have the same laws and customs.
2 a kind of club for people who like the same things. *A drama society.*

socket sockets *noun*
a thing in a wall with holes where you can push in an electric plug.

sofa sofas *noun*
a long, comfortable seat for two or more people, also called a settee.

soft softer softest *adjective*
1 not hard or rough. *Cats have soft fur.*
2 not firm or stiff. *Soft snow.*
3 not loud, quiet and gentle. *He has a soft voice.*
4 too kind. *The teacher is too soft, so her class is always noisy.*
softly *adverb*, **soften** *verb*
The butter is very hard because it has been in the refrigerator. We should leave it out to soften.

software *noun*
the part inside a computer or on a computer disk that has the instructions that make a computer work.

soil *noun*
the brown stuff, also called earth, that plants grow in.

solar *adjective*
to do with the Sun. *The Solar System.*

soldier soldiers *noun*
a person in an army. ▲ Say *sole-jer*

solid solids *noun*
an object that is hard and not a liquid or a gas. *Water is a liquid but ice is a solid.*

Pronunciation tip.

(**Exemplar material**)

Quick access method

Make sure alphabet wall strip is in view.

Hold dictionary closed between your palms, its spine on the table. With your thumbs, locate the halfway point and open — you should be in 'M'.

Ring or highlight letter 'M' on wall strip to show halfway mark. Decide whether you need to go on or back to find the letter you want.

Hold up first section of dictionary and locate halfway point as above — you should find letters 'D'/'E'. Repeat with second section — you should find letters 'R'/'S'.

Mark wall strip at 'D' and 'S' for quarter and three-quarter marks.

Explain how we can find any letter section by locating it on the alphabet strip, going in at the nearest marker and fine-tuning by turning on or back. Monitor the children to ensure all are turning pages gently and efficiently.

Pupil copymaster

Key words

fire	Pudding Lane
wooden	River Thames
diary	Samuel Pepys
thatch	baker's shop
London	weather
water	fire brigade
houses	citizens

Pupil copymaster

Index page

Key word	Page

(Exemplar material)

Checklists for alphabetically ordered texts

Example of a checklist for a dictionary

- Use the quick access method to find correct initial letter

- The key letter comes first

- Find the second letter in alphabetical order

- Definition follows

Example of a checklist for a glossary

- Use the quick access method to find correct letter section

- The key word comes first in bold

- Definition follows

Example of a checklist for an index

- List key words in alphabetical order, not page order

- Give the page number(s) next to the key word

- If there are lots of pages for a key word, list page numbers in order and separate using commas

- Place index at end of non-fiction text

Classworks Literacy Year 2 © Sara Moult, Nelson Thornes Ltd 2003

(Marking ladder)

Marking ladder for a glossary

Name: _____

Pupil	Objective	Teacher
	I listed the words in alphabetical order.	
	I used colour or bold print for the key word.	
	I explained the meaning clearly without using the word itself.	
	I put the word in a sample sentence.	
	I used highlighter or bold print for the key word in the main text.	
	What could I do to improve my glossary next time?	

(Pupil copymaster)

Marking ladder for an index

Name: _____

Pupil	Objective	Teacher
	I listed the key words and phrases in alphabetical order.	
	I put page number(s) after each key word and phrase.	
	I separated the page numbers with commas if there were two or more.	
	What could I do to improve my index next time?	

Stories with Familiar Settings 2

Outcome

A story based on a familiar setting

Objectives

Sentence

3 to recognise and take account of commas and exclamation marks in reading aloud with appropriate expression.

Text

3 to be aware of the difference between spoken and written language through comparing oral recounts with text; make use of formal story elements in retelling.

10 to use story structure to write about own experience in same/similar form.

11 to use language of time to structure a sequence of events, e.g. 'when I had finished ...', 'suddenly ...', 'after that ...'.

Improvisation

● adopt appropriate roles in small or large groups. Use texts as stimulus for dramatic interpretation.

Planning frame

● Telling, elaborating, planning and writing a humorous story (based on fact) in which things do not go according to plan.

● Talk for writing: retell the story using finger puppets; relate own true stories of humorous family incidents.

● Adapt and embellish true account orally.

● Story begins with direct speech.

● Written in the past tense.

● Direct speech carries the story forward.

● Time phrases move the story on.

● Title appears in text at beginning and end of story.

● Cover picture attracts attention and a visual representation of the contents.

How you could plan this unit

Day 1	Day 2	Day 3	Day 4	Day 5
Reading Introduce text (Resource Pages A and B) and read story	**Reading and analysis**	**Planning**	**Writing** The children produce own storyboard, using Resource Page F	**Reading and analysis** Reread opening, annotate and write a checklist (see Resource Pages C, D and G for ideas)
	Acting with Puppets	*Storyboarding*		

Day 6	Day 7	Day 8	Day 9	Day 10
Writing The children write story opening from plan using checklist	**Reading and analysis**	**Writing** The children write story middle from plan using checklist	**Reading and analysis** The children reread story ending, annotate and write a checklist (see Resource Pages D and G for ideas)	**Writing** The children write story ending from plan using checklist
	Moving the Story On			

Day 11	Day 12
Writing and evaluation Assess against marking ladder (Resource Page H) with response partners and rework chosen section	**Presentation** Share with audience. Dramatic presentation or with finger puppets

Acting with Puppets

Objective

We will retell the story in groups using puppets, noticing the differences between the written story and our retelling

You need: A copy of *A Quiet Night In* by Jill Murphy; Resource Pages A and B; fabric scraps and rubber bands for each group.

Whole class work

- Share-read to the end of the story (Resource Pages A and B show the start of the story). *Do you think it was an interesting story? Did it remind you of any other stories you have read? Who was your favourite character? Why?*

- Look back at all the direct speech. *Did you notice how much speech there is in this story? The speech moves the story on.*

- *Why do you think the author wrote so much direct speech (rather than in the third person/past tense)? How does this make you feel about the people who are speaking?*

- Introduce the term 'oral storytelling'.

Independent, pair or guided work

- In groups of six or less, the children retell the story using finger puppets.

- Making the finger puppets and performing for the whole class are not the purposes of the activity. Children who are otherwise reticent will often open up in this kind of activity, losing their self-consciousness because they are not 'being themselves'.

- Once the story is familiar the children can retell it, sequencing events and finding voices for their characters using their own words.

- A collection of material scraps and a few rubber bands allows each child to dress up a finger as a character from the story. Some groups may need guidance in assigning roles but allow the children to discuss and negotiate roles in their groups as they prepare. This activity can be done in pairs or threes, with fingers on both hands being 'dressed'.

- The children will probably move naturally from the dressing up/planning stage into performance without needing to be timed or moved on, but prompt them to begin if necessary. Suggest that they find a 'voice' for their character as they prepare.

- The narrative will be accessed at a deeper level through being acted out, becoming a real experience for the children and opening the way to hot seating later.

Plenary

- Skim-read the text again, noticing the sequence of events and characters' speeches.

- *Did you notice any differences between your version and the original text?*

Storyboarding

Objectives

We will learn how a storyboard can be used to plan a story. We will turn an experience of our own into a story

You need: Resource Pages A, B and E; whiteboard/flip chart and pens.

Whole class work

- Share-read/skim-read the text (Resource Pages A and B show the beginning of this text) to aid recall.

- The children think, pair, share to identify the main events of the story.

- Together, record the sequence on the board.

- Identify together where the middle and end sections begin, discussing how you identify these sections.

- Model writing a storyboard in four stages: beginning, end and two middle frames (Resource Page E). Explain how these are used in film-making so the director can plan the story.

- Ask the children to recall an incident at home where things did not turn out quite as planned!
    - *How would you tell this incident to a friend?*
    - *Where would you begin?*
    - *What would your listeners need to be told to help them understand your story?*
    - *Where would you end it?*
    - *What details would you include to make it funny?*
    - *Would you do special voices for the people in your story as you told it?*

- Allow the children a few minutes to think of a story to tell. For those struggling, suggest a topic heading, for example, 'The day I was late ...', 'A surprise trip ...'.

- 'Backwards' planning of this kind is a useful exercise once a text is familiar. This allows a plan or skeleton of the story to emerge and provides a model for the children's own planning as well as giving an insight into an author's process.

Independent, pair or guided work

- In pairs, the children tell each other their stories, using the following prompts:
    - *Listen carefully to the whole story first.*
    - *Ask any questions you need to help you understand.*
    - *Tell the storyteller your favourite part.*
    - *Suggest a way the storyteller could improve the story.*

Plenary

- The children think of three ways to improve their story, perhaps by embellishment:
    - stretching the truth
    - rolling two incidents into one
    - making the beginning and ending more exciting;
    or by pruning:
    - leaving out the boring bits
    - shrinking the timescale.

- Trail the next lesson when the children will use their storyboards to begin to turn oral stories into written ones.

Moving the Story On

Objectives

We will learn to use the language of time to structure events in a story. We will also learn to use speech to move a story on.

You need: Resource Pages A–D and G; OHTs; flip chart and marker pen.

Whole class work

- Using *A Quiet Night In*, encourage pairs of children to define where the middle of the story begins and ends. As they feed back their suggestions to the class, prompt them to justify their answers.

- Explain that the focus of today's lesson is to identify the ways an author can move a story on. **Why might this be necessary?**

- Share-read the middle of the text. Using response partners, invite the children to suggest what devices the author, Jill Murphy, has used to achieve this.

- Explain that one 'tool' for structuring events within a story is the use of time phrases, for example, 'that morning'. Invite a child to identify, then highlight, time phrases used in the shared text. Scribe further phrases that could be used in the children's own writing, for example, 'when I had finished...', 'suddenly...', 'after that...'.

- Explain that another way of carrying the story forwards is by using direct speech. Ask the children to focus on the following extract from the story:

> "We're all going to bed," said Lester.
> "So you can be quiet," said Laura.
> "Without us," said Luke.
> "Shhh," said the baby.
> "Happy Birthday," said Mrs Large. "Come and see the table."

- Encourage the children to discuss with a response partner what they notice about the way direct speech is represented in text. Ensure that they are clear that only the words actually said out loud by the character are put inside the speech marks.

- **Why did the author start a new line after Lester had finished speaking? Why didn't she start a new line after '"Happy Birthday," said Mrs Large...?'**

- Using the annotated text (Resource Pages C and D), compile a class checklist for writing the middle of a story (see checklist 2, Resource Page G for ideas).

Independent, pair or guided work

- Using the class checklist, the children write the middle of their own story with a familiar setting.

Plenary

- Photocopy one or two pieces of work on to OHTs and display (or enlarge on a photocopier). Invite the children to identify and highlight time phrases that have been used to move the story on.

- Write the following on a flip chart and invite the children to decide where the speech marks should go:

> Can we have a story before we go to bed? asked Luke.

A Quiet Night In

"I want you all in bed early tonight," said Mrs Large. "It's Daddy's birthday and we're going to have a quiet night in."

"Can we be there too?" asked Laura.

"No," said Mrs Large. "It wouldn't be quiet with you lot all charging about like a herd of elephants."

"But we are a herd of elephants," said Lester.

"Smartypants," said Mrs Large. "Come on now, coats on. It's time for school."

That evening, Mrs Large had the children bathed and in their pyjamas before they had even had their tea. They were all very cross.

"It's only half past four," said Lester.

"It's not even dark yet."

"It soon will be," said Mrs Large grimly.

After tea, the children set about making place cards and decorations for the dinner table. Then they all tidied up. Then Mrs Large tidied up again.

continued …

A Quiet Night In (continued)

Mr Large arrived home looking very tired.

"We're all going to bed," said Lester.

"So you can be quiet," said Laura.

"Without us," said Luke.

"Shhhh," said the baby.

"Happy Birthday," said Mrs Large. "Come and see the table."

Mr Large sank heavily into the sofa. "It's lovely, dear," he said, "but do you think we could have our dinner on trays in front of the TV? I'm feeling a bit tired."

"Of course," said Mrs Large. "It's your birthday. You can have whatever you want."

"We'll help," said Luke.

The children ran to the kitchen and brought two trays.

"I'll set them," said Mrs Large. "We don't want everything ending up on the floor."

"Can we have a story before we go to bed?" asked Luke.

"Please," said Lester.

"Go on, Dad," said Laura. "Just one."

"Story!" said the baby.

"Oh alright," said Mr Large. "Just one then." ...

Jill Murphy

(Exemplar analysis)

Example of analysis of *A Quiet Night In*

Direct speech to open story.

Title 'hidden' near story start.

Verbs in the past tense.

Time phrase moves the story on.

Time phrases and words move the story on.

"I want you all in bed early tonight," said Mrs Large. "It's Daddy's birthday and we're going to have a quiet night in."

"Can we be there too?" asked Laura.

"No," said Mrs Large. "It wouldn't be quiet with you lot all charging about like a herd of elephants."

"But we are a herd of elephants," said Lester.

"Smartypants," said Mrs Large. "Come on now, coats on. It's time for school."

That evening, Mrs Large had the children bathed and in their pyjamas before they had even had their tea. They were all very cross.

"It's only half past four," said Lester.

"It's not even dark yet."

"It soon will be," said Mrs Large grimly.

After tea, the children set about making place cards and decorations for the dinner table. Then they all tidied up. Then Mrs Large tidied up again.

continued …

(Exemplar analysis)

Example of analysis of *A Quiet Night In (continued)*

This character's catchphrase – watch for repetition.

Direct speech carries the story forwards.

Mr Large arrived home looking very tired.

"We're all going to bed," said Lester.

"So you can be quiet," said Laura.

"Without us," said Luke.

"Shhhh," said the baby.

"Happy Birthday," said Mrs Large. "Come and see the table."

Mr Large sank heavily into the sofa. "It's lovely, dear," he said, "but do you think we could have our dinner on trays in front of the TV? I'm feeling a bit tired."

"Of course," said Mrs Large. "It's your birthday. You can have whatever you want."

"We'll help," said Luke.

The children ran to the kitchen and brought two trays.

"I'll set them," said Mrs Large. "We don't want everything ending up on the floor."

"Can we have a story before we go to bed?" asked Luke.

"Please," said Lester.

"Go on, Dad," said Laura. "Just one."

"Story!" said the baby.

"Oh alright," said Mr Large. "Just one then." ...

Jill Murphy

(**Pupil copymaster**)

Modelled storyboard

1	2
Mrs Large and the children get things ready for Mr Large's birthday dinner.	Mr Large comes home tired and wants his dinner on a tray.

3	4
Mr Large reads the children a story and falls asleep on the sofa.	Mrs Large falls asleep, too. The children cover them both up and go to bed.

(**Pupil copymaster**)

Blank storyboard

1	2
3	4

(Exemplar material)

Checklists for stories with familiar settings

Example of a checklist for writing a story

- Use direct speech

- Write in the past tense

- Use time phrases

- Give it a clear beginning, middle and end

- 'Hide' the title at the beginning and end

Example of a checklist for the middle of a story

- Use time phrases to move the story on

- Use direct speech, ensuring that the speech marks " " go around the words spoken by the character

- Start a new line when a new character speaks

- Give one character a catchphrase that they repeat through the story

- Write in the past tense throughout the story

Marking ladder

Name: _____

Pupil	Objective	Teacher
	My story begins with direct speech.	
	I wrote in the past tense.	
	I used direct speech to carry the story forward.	
	I used time phrases to move the story on.	
	My story has a clear beginning, middle and ending.	
	I have 'hidden' my title at the beginning and end of my story.	
	What could I do to improve my story next time?	

Traditional Tales

Outcome

A dramatic improvisation of 'Little Red Riding Hood', using finger, sock or stick puppets; own written version of 'Little Red Riding Hood'

Objectives

Sentence

6 to identify speech marks in reading, understand their purpose, use the terms correctly.

8 to use commas to separate items in a list.

Text

3 to discuss and compare story theme.

7 to prepare and retell stories individually and through role-play in groups, using dialogue and narrative from text.

Speaking and listening

- to use role-play and improvisation to represent characters.

- watching others' plays and presentations: describe what characters are like; identify aspects of the performance they enjoyed.

Planning frame

- Read or tell traditional tales and build list of key features.

- Perform with puppets and discuss others' performances.

- Analyse written tales and build checklists, including different versions.

- Write own stories using checklists.

How you could plan this unit

Day 1	Day 2	Day 3	Day 4	Day 5
Analysis Revisit traditional tales, identify key features, retell known versions of *Little Red Riding Hood*	**Application** Performance in groups with puppets. Response to others' performance	**Reading and analysis** *Talking about Themes*	**Reading and analysis** *Story Openings*	**Application** Demonstrate writing a story opening using the plan from Day 3. The children write the beginning of their story independently

Day 6	Day 7	Day 8	Day 9	Day 10
Reading and analysis *Different Versions*	**Writing** Demonstrate writing story middle using plan from Day 3. The children write their story middle independently	**Reading and analysis** Read story ending (Resource Page C), build checklist. Compare and annotate different versions of middle/ending	**Writing** Demonstrate writing story ending using plan from Day 3 and checklist. The children write their story ending independently	**Evaluation** The children evaluate work using marking ladder (Resource Page K)

Talking about Themes

Objective

We will think and talk about a story theme, then plan a different version of the same story

You need: Resource Pages A–C or big book version of *Little Red Riding Hood*, by Jonathan Langley (Collins Educational); Resource Page G; flip chart.

Whole class work

- Together read the shared text (Resource Pages A–C), asking the children to note differences with other familiar versions of *Little Red Riding Hood*.

- Record differences on a flip chart. These might include:

character's name	no detail of basket contents
character description (grumpy)	Granny's fate (she is sometimes locked in a cupboard rather than eaten)
no use of speech: "Lift up the latch and come in"	
	Mother's appearance at end of story

- Model planning a different version of the story. Introduce the changes you might make and record as a flow chart, for example:
  - make Little Red Riding Hood cheerful and helpful
  - introduce another character – a talking cat for a companion; the cat reminds Little Red Riding Hood of mother's warnings
  - change meeting between wolf and Little Red Riding Hood – wolf poses as lost traveller asking the way out of the wood
  - change Grandma's fate – wolf ties her up with her own knitting wool and drops her in the dustbin
  - change fate of wolf – wolf flees in terror when talking cat impersonates woodcutter's voice from inside a cupboard
  - change final scene – Little Red Riding Hood, Grandma and the cat sit down to tea and cakes from the basket.

Independent, pair or guided work

- In pairs, the children talk through the changes they would like to make to the story to produce their own version. They then record their ideas on a story flow chart (Resource Page G). Pairs may use the same plan but will write independently.

Plenary

- Draw the children's attention to the common threads in all versions:
  - *Is this really the story of Little Red Riding Hood?*
  - *How do you know it is the same story?*
  - *Why do you think different versions exist?*
  - *What does Little Red Riding Hood learn from the experience?*
  - *What are we supposed to learn?*

- Introduce the term 'theme' for the idea behind a story.

- In most versions, Little Red Riding Hood lives on the edge of a forest and must go deeper into the forest alone, relying on her mother's advice. The children should be able, with help, to see that the story is about growing up, becoming independent, remembering advice, staying safe. It is the original 'stranger danger' story!

- Note themes on flip chart.

100

Story Openings

Objectives

We will learn to annotate a story opening, building a checklist. We will also learn to compare and contrast different versions of the same story

You need: Resource Pages A–D and H–J; alternative versions of *Little Red Riding Hood*.

Whole class work

- Using an enlarged copy of the shared text (Resource Pages A–C), invite the children to reread the story, then identify with a partner where the story opening begins and ends. As they feed back their ideas, challenge them to justify their decisions.

- Having defined the story opening, begin to discuss what type of information is detailed in this part of the story, for example, a traditional story opening is used, the character is introduced, and so on. Annotate the text appropriately (see Resource Page D), then compile the key features into a class checklist (see checklist 1, Resource Page J for ideas).

- Referring to the checklist, begin to scribe alternative ideas for each of the key points, for example different traditional story openings ('One day …', 'A long time ago …'); different settings ('On the edge of a deep, dark lake', 'On the tall cliffs by the raging ocean'); these can be added to the checklist to support the children when writing their own version in the next lesson.

- Remind the children that there are many different versions of *Little Red Riding Hood*. Using an enlarged copy of the comparison grid (Resource Page H), invite the children to scan the text for the answers to questions 1–5 (the story opening). Scribe their answers in the column headed 'Jonathan Langley version' (see Resource Page I).

Independent, pair or guided work

- Using an alternative version of *Little Red Riding Hood* the children annotate the opening of the story as demonstrated in the shared session. If resources permit, you may like to have a different version of the text for each group. The children should work in pairs at this stage.

- The children then use the comparison grid to compare and contrast the opening in their version of the text with that by Jonathan Langley.

Plenary

- Using their comparison grids, invite the children to feed back the answers to questions 1–5 for the alternative version of the text they annotated in the independent session.

- The answers can be added to the class comparison grid and used as an aid for comparing and contrasting several versions of the text.

Different Versions

Objectives

We will build a checklist for writing the middle of a traditional story. We will also develop our ability to compare and contrast different versions of the same story

You need: Resource Pages A–C, E, F, I and J; flip chart and pens; whiteboards; alternative versions of *Little Red Riding Hood* from school and home.

Whole class work

- Using an enlarged copy of the shared text (Resource Pages A–C), invite the children to recall where the middle of the story begins and identify where they think it ends.

- Ask the children to reread the middle of the story carefully with a partner and identify key features to be annotated. You may like to prompt the children with questions such as:
  - *How are the characters developed?*
  - *What features does the writer use to hold the reader's interest?*
  - *What is the effect of using the patterned language "What big ... you've got"/ "All the better..."?*

- Select children to share their ideas, then invite them to annotate the text appropriately (see Resource Pages E and F).

- Begin to incorporate these key features into a class checklist for writing the middle of a traditional tale (see checklist 2, Resource Page J).

- Using the enlarged copy of the class comparison grid partially completed in the previous lesson (Resource Page I), invite the children to scribe the answers to questions 6–8 on their whiteboards. Discuss their ideas before scribing them in the column headed 'Jonathan Langley version'.

Independent, pair or guided work

- Using an alternative version of *Little Red Riding Hood*, the children independently annotate the middle of the story as demonstrated in the shared session.

- The children then use the comparison grid to compare and contrast the middle of the story in their version of the text with that by Jonathan Langley.

Plenary

- Drawing together the children's findings from the independent session, continue to fill in the class comparison grid.

- Discuss some of the differences between the versions. *Why do you think the writer added/omitted this piece of information? Which version do you prefer and why?*

(Pupil copymaster)

Little Red Riding Hood

Once upon a time, on the edge of the big wood, there lived a little girl called Little Red Riding Hood. Her real name was Brenda but she was always known as Little Red Riding Hood because this was what her mother called her when she was a baby. Brenda used to wear a red bonnet when she went out for a ride in her pram, and she still wears it now.

One day Little Red Riding Hood was playing out in the sunshine when her mother called her. "I want you to go over to Grandma's house with some groceries. Grandma's not very well and she hasn't been able to get out to the shops."

"Do I have to?" said Little Red Riding Hood with a glum face.

"Yes you do!" said Mum. "Now go and wash your face."

Mum packed the groceries into a basket while Little Red Riding Hood did as she was told.

When the basket was ready Mum looked at Little Red Riding Hood very seriously, "Now I want you to be very sensible," she said. "Don't mess about. Stay on the path and don't talk to any strangers."

She kissed Little Red Riding Hood on top of her head, handed her the basket of groceries, and pushed her out of the door. Little Red Riding Hood scowled and stomped off down the path into the wood.

Little Red Riding Hood hadn't been walking far when she heard a rustling in the trees. Then she heard a deep, silky voice calling, "Little girl, little girl, can you spare a minute?"

Little Red Riding Hood was curious and strayed off the path to see where the voice was coming from. It seemed to come from the dark shadows behind the trees. There was a funny smell of old dogs and, for a moment, she thought she saw a tall woolly figure. She remembered what her mum had said but the voice was quite friendly. "What do you want?" said Little Red Riding Hood boldly.

"Where are you going, little girl?" said the voice.

"I'm going to Grandma's house. She's not well and I'm taking her some groceries," said Little Red Riding Hood.

"How kind," said the voice. "What a good girl you must be. And where does your poor grandmother live?"

Little Red Riding Hood smiled angelically and replied in her sweetest voice, "She lives at the far side of the wood, next to the pond."

continued …

(Pupil copymaster)

Little Red Riding Hood (2)

"What a pleasant place to live," said the soft voice, "but we mustn't keep the old lady waiting. Off you go, dear."

Little Red Riding Hood waved and continued on to Grandma's house.

When Little Red Riding Hood was out of sight the tall woolly figure stepped out of the shadows and smiled a big sharp-toothed smile.

The silky voice belonged to a wolf!

He was hungry and wanted to eat Little Red Riding Hood but he was also clever. He was too near the little girl's house and her mother might hear her scream. If he took the short cut through the trees, he thought, he could arrive at Grandma's house before Little Red Riding Hood, and then he could eat the tasty little girl and her fat old grandmother. Licking his lips he raced off into the dark wood.

When the wolf reached Grandma's house he sneaked round the back and peeked in through the kitchen window. Grandma was making a pot of tea. The wolf lifted the latch silently and tip-toed in when Grandma's back was turned. Then, before Grandma could shout, 'tea-bag!' the greedy wolf swallowed her whole.

"Mmm, yum, yum," he said. Then, he hurried to Grandma's bedroom and searched her drawers until he found a big pink nightgown and a frilly nightcap.

Quickly the wolf dressed himself in Grandma's clothes and leapt into bed just as he heard Little Red Riding Hood approaching the house.

"Grandma, where are you?" shouted Little Red Riding Hood.

"I'm in bed, child," called the wolf in his best 'old lady' voice. "Come right in, the door's not locked."

Little Red Riding Hood opened the back door and stepped into the kitchen. There was a funny smell which was different from Grandma's smell, and the teapot lay broken on the floor.

"Grandma, are you alright?" called Little Red Riding Hood.

"Yes dear, I'm not feeling myself today so I decided to go back to bed. Do come in and see me."

It was dark in Grandma's room because the curtains were drawn. Little Red Riding Hood, still holding the basket of groceries, stood beside the bed. How strange, she thought, there was that funny smell of old dogs again. She looked at the figure under the great heap of bedclothes and frowned.

"Grandma, are you sure you're alright?" said Little Red Riding Hood.

"Of course, my child. I'm just a bit under the weather," said the wolf.

Little Red Riding Hood thought Grandma's voice sounded strange, but she did have a bad cold. Then she noticed Grandma's ears.

continued …

(Pupil copymaster)

Little Red Riding Hood (3)

"Grandma, what big ears you have!"

"All the better to hear you with, my dear," said the wolf.

Then Little Red Riding Hood noticed Grandma's gleaming eyes.

"Grandma, what big eyes you have!"

"All the better to see you with, my dear," said the wolf.

Then as Little Red Riding Hood's eyes became accustomed to the dim light, she noticed Grandma's pointed nose and shining teeth.

"Grandma, what big teeth you have!"

At this point the wolf leapt up and growled, "ALL THE BETTER TO EAT YOU WITH, MY DEAR!"

The wolf's jaws were all around but, quick as a flash, Little Red Riding Hood swung the shopping basket and hit the wolf squarely on the nose. He yelped and fell back.

At that moment the door burst open and there stood Mum with Grandma's frying pan in her hand! She lifted it high above her head, then brought it down with a CLANG! on the wicked wolf's head.

He did not move again.

Little Red Riding Hood ran to her mother who hugged her tight. "Mum, why are you here?" she said.

"I had a funny feeling in my bones," said Mum, "so I decided to come and see how Grandma was for myself. Where is she?"

There was a muffled cry from where the wolf was lying and something was moving in the wolf's tummy!

"Quick, Little Red Riding Hood, get the scissors," said Mum. With a snip, snip, snip, Mum cut open the wolf's tummy and out spilled an angry Grandma. She was shaken but, luckily, not harmed in any way.

"I'm going to teach that wolf a lesson," said Grandma. "Fetch me my sewing basket, Little Red Riding Hood."

Grandma worked quickly. From under the kitchen sink she pulled a sack of onions. She stuffed them all into the wolf's tummy then, with her best embroidery stitches, sewed up the woolly beast's belly. Then Grandma, Mum and Little Red Riding Hood together rolled the sleeping wolf across the floor and out of the door. Grandma slammed the door shut.

"Put the kettle on, Little Red Riding Hood, what we need now is a cup of tea," said Grandma, who was feeling much better.

When the wolf woke up he felt terrible. His head hurt and his tummy felt as though it was on fire. "Oooh," he said to himself, "I'll never eat another grandma again."

And he never did, and he never talked to strange girls again either.

Jonathan Langley

(Exemplar analysis)

Example of analysis of *Little Red Riding Hood*

Traditional story opening.

Setting.

Explanation of character's nickname.

Narrative begins.

Direct speech sets up task, introduces new character, gives more detail of Little Red Riding Hood character.

Mother's warning.

Powerful verb tells the reader how the character is feeling.

Wolf 'hidden' from reader – introduced by sound and smell.

Description of a glimpse.

Opening makes you want to read on.

Once upon a time, on the edge of the big wood, there lived a little girl called Little Red Riding Hood. Her real name was Brenda but she was always known as Little Red Riding Hood because this was what her mother called her when she was a baby. Brenda used to wear a red bonnet when she went out for a ride in her pram, and she still wears it now.

One day Little Red Riding Hood was playing out in the sunshine when her mother called her. "I want you to go over to Grandma's house with some groceries. Grandma's not very well and she hasn't been able to get out to the shops."

"Do I have to?" said Little Red Riding Hood with a glum face.

"Yes you do!" said Mum. "Now go and wash your face."

Mum packed the groceries into a basket while Little Red Riding Hood did as she was told.

When the basket was ready Mum looked at Little Red Riding Hood very seriously, "Now I want you to be very sensible," she said. "Don't mess about. Stay on the path and don't talk to any strangers."

She kissed Little Red Riding Hood on top of her head, handed her the basket of groceries, and pushed her out of the door. Little Red Riding Hood scowled and stomped off down the path into the wood.

Little Red Riding Hood hadn't been walking far when she heard a rustling in the trees. Then she heard a deep, silky voice calling, "Little girl, little girl, can you spare a minute?"

Little Red Riding Hood was curious and strayed off the path to see where the voice was coming from. It seemed to come from the dark shadows behind the trees. There was a funny smell of old dogs and, for a moment, she thought she saw a tall woolly figure. She remembered what her mum had said but the voice was quite friendly.

"What do you want?" said Little Red Riding Hood boldly.

"Where are you going, little girl?" said the voice.

"I'm going to Grandma's house. She's not well and I'm taking her some groceries," said Little Red Riding Hood.

"How kind," said the voice. "What a good girl you must be. And where does your poor grandmother live?"

Little Red Riding Hood smiled angelically and replied in her sweetest voice, "She lives at the far side of the wood, next to the pond."

continued ...

(Exemplar analysis)

Example of analysis of *Little Red Riding Hood (2)*

Direct speech moves the story on.

Story splits here – 'meanwhile' episode begins.

Character finally revealed to reader (but not to Little Red Riding Hood).

Details of wolf's wicked plan – known to reader but hidden from Little Red Riding Hood.

Clues understood by reader but not by Little Red Riding Hood – reader knows more than the character in the story.

"What a pleasant place to live," said the soft voice, "but we mustn't keep the old lady waiting. Off you go, dear."

Little Red Riding Hood waved and continued on to Grandma's house.

When Little Red Riding Hood was out of sight the tall woolly figure stepped out of the shadows and smiled a big sharp-toothed smile.

The silky voice belonged to a wolf!

He was hungry and wanted to eat Little Red Riding Hood but he was also clever. He was too near the little girl's house and her mother might hear her scream. If he took the short cut through the trees, he thought, he could arrive at Grandma's house before Little Red Riding Hood, and then he could eat the tasty little girl and her fat old grandmother. Licking his lips he raced off into the dark wood.

When the wolf reached Grandma's house he sneaked round the back and peeked in through the kitchen window. Grandma was making a pot of tea. The wolf lifted the latch silently and tip-toed in when Grandma's back was turned. Then, before Grandma could shout, 'tea-bag!' the greedy wolf swallowed her whole.

"Mmm, yum, yum," he said. Then, he hurried to Grandma's bedroom and searched her drawers until he found a big pink nightgown and a frilly nightcap.

Quickly the wolf dressed himself in Grandma's clothes and leapt into bed just as he heard Little Red Riding Hood approaching the house.

"Grandma, where are you?" shouted Little Red Riding Hood.

"I'm in bed, child," called the wolf in his best 'old lady' voice. "Come right in, the door's not locked."

Little Red Riding Hood opened the back door and stepped into the kitchen. There was a funny smell which was different from Grandma's smell, and the teapot lay broken on the floor.

"Grandma, are you alright?" called Little Red Riding Hood.

"Yes dear, I'm not feeling myself today so I decided to go back to bed. Do come in and see me."

It was dark in Grandma's room because the curtains were drawn. Little Red Riding Hood, still holding the basket of groceries, stood beside the bed. How strange, she thought, there was that funny smell of old dogs again. She looked at the figure under the great heap of bedclothes and frowned.

"Grandma, are you sure you're alright?" said Little Red Riding Hood.

"Of course, my child. I'm just a bit under the weather," said the wolf.

Little Red Riding Hood thought Grandma's voice sounded strange, but she did have a bad cold. Then she noticed Grandma's ears.

continued …

(Exemplar analysis)

Example of analysis of *Little Red Riding Hood (3)*

Repetitive, patterned speeches.

End of middle section – beginning of end!

Little Red Riding Hood and her mother save the day themselves!

Mum rescues Grandma.

Grandma gets revenge on the wolf.

Wolf is punished – reader knows more than character again.

Twist on usual message!

"Grandma, what big ears you have!"

"All the better to hear you with, my dear," said the wolf.

Then Little Red Riding Hood noticed Grandma's gleaming eyes.

"Grandma, what big eyes you have!"

"All the better to see you with, my dear," said the wolf.

Then as Little Red Riding Hood's eyes became accustomed to the dim light, she noticed Grandma's pointed nose and shining teeth.

"Grandma, what big teeth you have!"

At this point the wolf leapt up and growled, "ALL THE BETTER TO EAT YOU WITH, MY DEAR!"

The wolf's jaws were all around but, quick as a flash, Little Red Riding Hood swung the shopping basket and hit the wolf squarely on the nose. He yelped and fell back.

At that moment the door burst open and there stood Mum with Grandma's frying pan in her hand! She lifted it high above her head, then brought it down with a CLANG! on the wicked wolf's head.

He did not move again.

Little Red Riding Hood ran to her mother who hugged her tight. "Mum, why are you here?" she said.

"I had a funny feeling in my bones," said Mum, "so I decided to come and see how Grandma was for myself. Where is she?"

There was a muffled cry from where the wolf was lying and something was moving in the wolf's tummy!

"Quick, Little Red Riding Hood, get the scissors," said Mum. With a snip, snip, snip, Mum cut open the wolf's tummy and out spilled an angry Grandma. She was shaken but, luckily, not harmed in any way.

"I'm going to teach that wolf a lesson," said Grandma. "Fetch me my sewing basket, Little Red Riding Hood."

Grandma worked quickly. From under the kitchen sink she pulled a sack of onions. She stuffed them all into the wolf's tummy then, with her best embroidery stitches, sewed up the woolly beast's belly. Then Grandma, Mum and Little Red Riding Hood together rolled the sleeping wolf across the floor and out of the door. Grandma slammed the door shut.

"Put the kettle on, Little Red Riding Hood, what we need now is a cup of tea," said Grandma, who was feeling much better.

When the wolf woke up he felt terrible. His head hurt and his tummy felt as though it was on fire. "Oooh," he said to himself, "I'll never eat another grandma again."

And he never did, and he never talked to strange girls again either.

Jonathan Langley

Pupil copymaster

Story flow chart

Introduce 'goodie' (Little Red Riding Hood)

Set up journey/challenge/task (trip to Grandma's)

Introduce 'baddie' who meets goodie (wolf)

| Goodie carries on with journey ... | MEANWHILE ... | Baddie carries out evil plan (wolf eats Grandma) |

Goodie and baddie meet up again = conflict (Little Red Riding Hood and wolf at Grandma's)

Resolution of conflict = goodie wins (Little Red Riding Hood safe, wolf taught a lesson)

Pupil copymaster

Comparison grid

Story feature	Jonathan Langley version	Version 2	Version 3	Version 4
1. How did Little Red Riding Hood get her name?				
2. Where does she live?				
3. What is her mother's advice?				
4. What is her task?				
5. What must she take?				
6. How is the wolf introduced?				
7. Any repeated speeches?				
8. What happens to Grandma?				
9. Who rescues Little Red Riding Hood?				
10. What happens to the wolf?				

(Exemplar material)

Modelled comparison grid

Story feature	Jonathan Langley version	Version 2	Version 3	Version 4
1. How did Little Red Riding Hood get her name?	Wears a red baby bonnet			
2. Where does she live?	Edge of a big wood			
3. What is her mother's advice?	Go straight through the wood, stay on the path, don't talk to strangers			
4. What is her task?	To take groceries to her Grandma			
5. What must she take?	Not specified			
6. How is the wolf introduced?	Smelly, silky voice, shadow behind trees			
7. Any repeated speeches?	"Grandma, what big ..." "All the better to ..."			
8. What happens to Grandma?	Eaten by wolf			
9. Who rescues Little Red Riding Hood?	Herself and her mother			
10. What happens to the wolf?	Alive with a tummy full of onions!			

(Exemplar material)

Checklists for traditional tales

Checklist for writing the opening of *Little Red Riding Hood* ①

- Use a traditional story start
- Introduce the setting ('on the edge of a big wood')
- Introduce and describe the character
- Give the good character a task to complete
- Make the reader want to read on

Checklist for writing the middle of *Little Red Riding Hood* ②

- Use direct speech
- Maintain the reader's interest with descriptions, for example, 'a deep, silky voice'
- Little Red Riding Hood ignores her mother's advice
- Repeat the speech "Grandma, what big … you have!"/"All the better to … you with, my dear"

Checklist for writing the end of *Little Red Riding Hood* ③

- The problem is resolved
- Little Red Riding Hood and Grandma are safe
- Something happens to the wolf
- The wolf repents
- Use a traditional story ending

(**Marking ladder**)

Name: _____

Pupil	Objective	Teacher
	I used a traditional story start.	
	I introduced and described Little Red Riding Hood.	
	I described the setting.	
	I introduced her task using direct speech.	
	I described her journey through the forest.	
	I introduced and described the wolf.	
	I detailed the meeting between the wolf and Little Red Riding Hood using direct speech.	
	I used repetitive language.	
	I resolved the problem satisfactorily.	
	I used a traditional story ending.	
	What could I do to improve my tale next time?	

Poems by Walter de la Mare

Outcome

A poem using the structure of a known poem

Objectives	**Sentence**
	2 to read aloud with intonation and expression appropriate to the grammar and punctuation.
	Text
	8 to read own poems aloud.
	9 to identify and discuss patterns of rhythm, rhyme and other features of sound in different poems.
	10 to comment on and recognise when the reading aloud of a poem makes sense and is effective.
	11 to identify and discuss favourite poems and poets, using appropriate terms ('poet', 'poem', 'verse', 'rhyme', etc.) and referring to the language of the poems.
	15 to use structures from poems as a basis for writing, by extending or substituting elements, inventing own lines, verses; to make class collections, illustrate with captions; to write own poems from initial jottings and words.
Planning frame	● Read and analyse poems by Walter de la Mare.
	● Build checklist of features.
	● Write a new stanza for one poem.
	● Discuss and improve writing with a partner.
Note	● This unit is based on poems by the well-known children's poet Walter de la Mare. The children will read and perform one or more of these poems and be encouraged to learn at least one by heart.

How you could plan this unit

Day 1	Day 2	Day 3	Day 4	Day 5
Reading and analysis	Reading and analysis The children read, annotate and learn by heart *Some One* (Resource Pages G and H)	Reading and analysis The children read and annotate *Bunches of Grapes* (Resource Pages I and J). Develop checklist (see Resource Page O for ideas)	Writing	Writing Polish stanza(s) with response partner. Choose own or other poem to learn by heart. Perform poem (optional)
Finding Patterns			*A New Stanza*	

Finding Patterns

Objectives

We will find patterns of words and sound in different poems and read them aloud. We will learn a poem by heart and recite it to an audience

You need: Resource Pages A–F and K–M.

Whole class work

- Introduce the poem *Eeka, Neeka* (Resource Page A). Ask the children to look first at the shape it makes on the page without reading it.

- *Do you know what this is?* Think, pair, share to arrive at the answer: 'a poem'.

- *How can you tell?*

- *Find evidence to support your view:*
  - lines begin with capital letters
  - lines don't always end with full stops
  - not written in sentences
  - lines don't reach to the edge of the page.

- Read the poem aloud to the children.

- Don't be tempted to rely on individual copies held by each child. The text may be identical but the children are isolated with their copies and cannot share the experience of reading and annotating.

- Discuss:
  - *How does this poem make you feel?*
  - *What pictures do you see in your mind?*
  - *Who is the poet talking to?*
  - *Why are the last two lines in a separate stanza?*
  - *What does the title mean?*

- Annotate the text together (see Resource Page B).

Independent, pair or guided work

- In pairs, the children read and annotate another Walter de la Mare poem, either *The Snowflake* (Resource Pages C and D) or *Ice* (Resource Pages E and F) and learn it by heart, ready to perform to a partner, their group or the whole class. (See Resource Page M for tips on helping the children to memorise poems.)

- Guided read, analyse and annotate another poem from this unit (Resource Pages K and L).

Plenary

- Use this opportunity for performance of the learned poem. Try a 'Walk to talk' if the children have been working in pairs: everyone gets up and moves to find a different partner with whom they can share their poem.

- Go round the different groups, or ask the children to nominate an especially good performance from another child. This avoids the need to hear 30 performances of the same poem!

- Homework could be to recite the learned poem to someone at home.

A New Stanza

Objective

We will invent more stanzas for the poem *Bunches of Grapes*

You need: Resource Pages I and N–P.

Whole class work	• Revisit *Bunches of Grapes* (Resource Page I) and look at the class checklist built in the previous lesson (based on Resource Page O).
	• Model writing a new stanza (see Resource Page O for ideas). The children assess your stanza against the checklist.
	• Count the syllables to check that the modelled writing matches the original stanzas.
	• Keep original names or use rhyming names from the class. The names have three syllables, two syllables and one syllable respectively. The two-syllable name needs the stress to fall on its second syllable. The second and third names must rhyme.
	• *Why does the last line have to be so much longer?*
	• The children read the old and new stanzas, clapping the beats in each line as they go.
	• *What favourite things could we base a new stanza on?* For example, toys, games, weather, clothes, songs.
Independent, pair or guided work	• The children write a new stanza (or two) for the poem, using the class checklist and the writing frame (Resource Page N).
	• A selection of stanzas on different topics, including your modelled writing, can be strung together to make a class version of the poem. This could become an illustrated poetry book for the class library or for sharing with another class.
	• The children share their work with a response partner using the marking ladder (Resource Page P).
Plenary	• Use this opportunity for performance of the new stanza with a 'Walk to talk'. Everyone gets up and moves to find a different partner to share their poem with.
	• Again, ask the children to nominate an especially good performance from another child.

(Pupil copymaster)

Eeka, Neeka

Eeka, Neeka, Leeka, Lee,

Here's a lock without a key;

Bring a lantern, bring a candle,

Here's a door without a handle,

Shine, shine, you old thief Moon,

Here's a door without a room;

Not a whisper, moth or mouse,

Key – lock – door – room: where's the house?

Say nothing, creep away,

And live to knock another day!

Walter de la Mare (1873–1956)

Exemplar analysis

Example of analysis of *Eeka, Neeka*

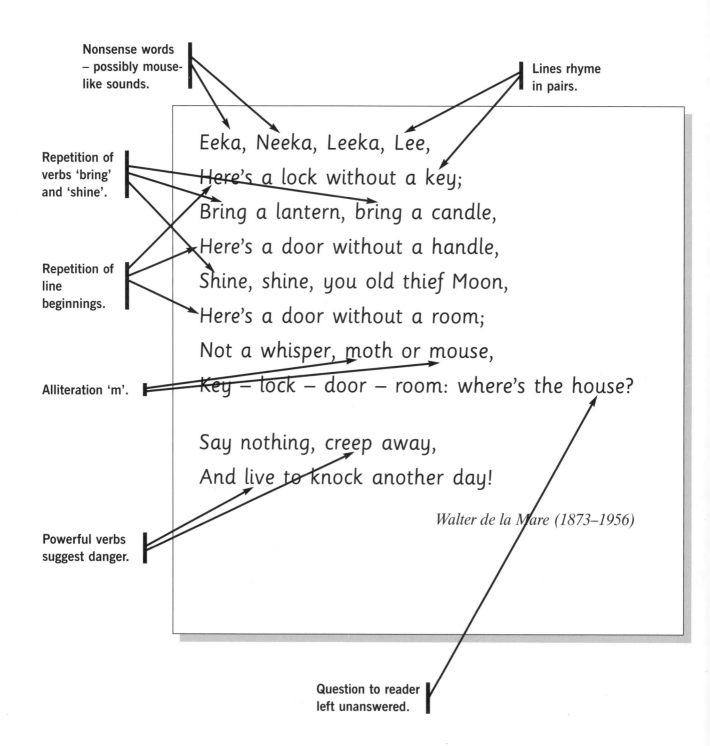

Nonsense words – possibly mouse-like sounds.

Lines rhyme in pairs.

Repetition of verbs 'bring' and 'shine'.

Repetition of line beginnings.

Alliteration 'm'.

Powerful verbs suggest danger.

Question to reader left unanswered.

Eeka, Neeka, Leeka, Lee,

Here's a lock without a key;

Bring a lantern, bring a candle,

Here's a door without a handle,

Shine, shine, you old thief Moon,

Here's a door without a room;

Not a whisper, moth or mouse,

Key – lock – door – room: where's the house?

Say nothing, creep away,

And live to knock another day!

Walter de la Mare (1873–1956)

The Snowflake

Before I melt,

Come look at me!

This lovely icy filigree!

Of a great forest

In one night

I make a wilderness

Of white:

By skyey cold

Of crystals made,

All softly, on

Your finger laid.

I pause, that you

My beauty see:

Breathe, and I vanish

Instantly.

Walter de la Mare

(Exemplar analysis)

Example of analysis of *The Snowflake*

Before I melt,

Come look at me!

This lovely icy filigree!

Of a great forest   A

In one night   B

I make a wilderness   C

Of white: B

By skyey cold   A

Of crystals made,   B

All softly, on   C

Your finger laid.   B

I pause, that you   A

My beauty see: B

Breathe, and I vanish   C

Instantly.   B

Walter de la Mare

Rhyming couplet, then ABCB rhyme pattern for the rest of the poem

Discussion point: Who is the 'I' in the poem? (The poet gives the snowflake a voice!)

Pupil copymaster

Ice

The North wind sighed:
And in a trice
What was water
Now is ice.

What sweet rippling water was
Now bewitched is
Into glass:

White and brittle
Where is seen
The prisoned milfoil's
Tender green;

Clear and ringing
With sun aglow,
Where the boys sliding
And skating go.

Now furred's each stick
And stalk and blade
With crystals out of
Dewdrops made.

Worms and ants
Flies, snails and bees
Keep close house-guard
Lest they freeze;

Oh, with how sad
And solemn an eye
Each fish stares up
Into the sky.

In dread lest his
Wide watery home
At night shall solid
Ice become.

Walter de la Mare

Exemplar analysis

Example of analysis of *Ice*

The North wind sighed:
And in a trice
What was water
Now is ice.

What/sweet rippling water was
/Now bewitched is
Into glass:

White and brittle
Where is seen
The prisoned milfoil's
Tender green;

Clear and ringing
With sun aglow,
Where the boys/sliding
And skating go.

Now furred's each stick
And stalk and blade
With crystals/out of
Dewdrops made.

Worms and ants
Flies, snails and bees
Keep close house-guard
Lest they freeze;

Oh, with how sad
And solemn an eye
Each fish stares up
Into the sky.

In dread lest his
Wide watery home
At night shall/solid
Ice become.

Walter de la Mare

Note use of unusual word order to fit the pattern of the short lines.

/ indicates where the verb might normally be expected to go.

Discussion point:
Why do you think the poet used this unusual word order? What effect does it have?

Some One

Some one came knocking
At my wee, small door;
Some one came knocking,
I'm sure, sure, sure;
I listened, I opened,
I looked to left and right,
But nought there was a-stirring
In the still dark night;
Only the busy beetle
Tap-tapping in the wall,
Only from the forest
The screech-owl's call,
Only the cricket whistling
While the dewdrops fall,
So I know not who came knocking,
At all, at all, at all.

Walter de la Mare

Exemplar analysis

Example of analysis of *Some One*

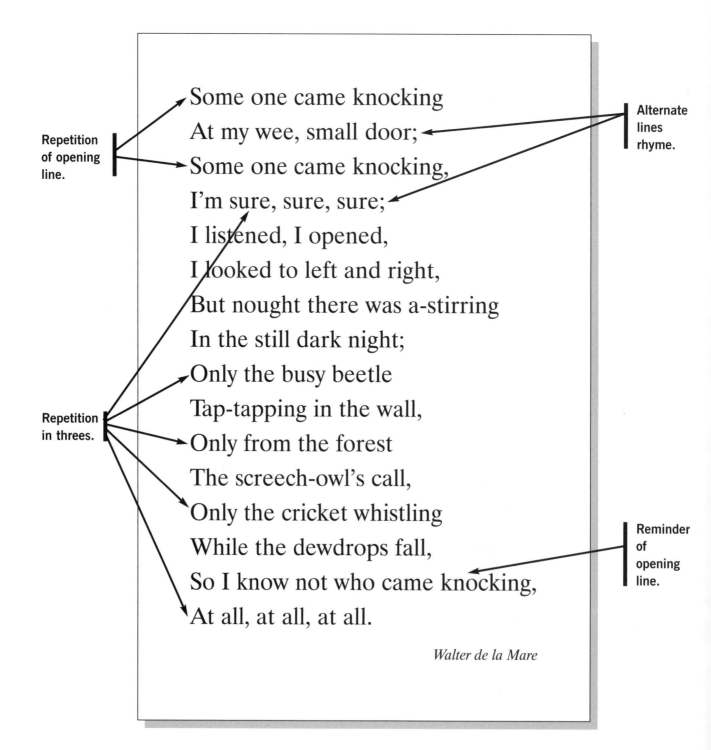

Some one came knocking
At my wee, small door;
Some one came knocking,
I'm sure, sure, sure;
I listened, I opened,
I looked to left and right,
But nought there was a-stirring
In the still dark night;
Only the busy beetle
Tap-tapping in the wall,
Only from the forest
The screech-owl's call,
Only the cricket whistling
While the dewdrops fall,
So I know not who came knocking,
At all, at all, at all.

Walter de la Mare

Repetition of opening line.

Repetition in threes.

Alternate lines rhyme.

Reminder of opening line.

Bunches of Grapes

"Bunches of grapes," says Timothy;
"Pomegranates pink," says Elaine;
"A junket of cream and a cranberry tart
"For me," says Jane.

"Love-in-a-mist," says Timothy;
"Primroses pale," says Elaine;
"A nosegay of pinks and mignonette
"For me," says Jane.

"Chariots of gold," says Timothy;
"Silvery wings," says Elaine;
"A bumpety ride in a wagon of hay
"For me," says Jane.

Walter de la Mare

Exemplar analysis

Example of analysis of *Bunches of Grapes*

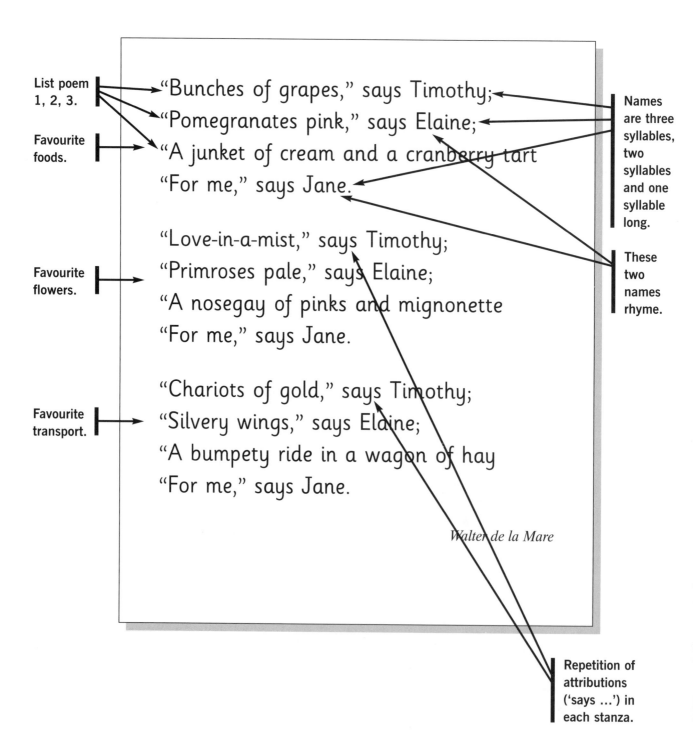

List poem 1, 2, 3.

Favourite foods.

Favourite flowers.

Favourite transport.

"Bunches of grapes," says Timothy;

"Pomegranates pink," says Elaine;

"A junket of cream and a cranberry tart

"For me," says Jane.

"Love-in-a-mist," says Timothy;

"Primroses pale," says Elaine;

"A nosegay of pinks and mignonette

"For me," says Jane.

"Chariots of gold," says Timothy;

"Silvery wings," says Elaine;

"A bumpety ride in a wagon of hay

"For me," says Jane.

Walter de la Mare

Names are three syllables, two syllables and one syllable long.

These two names rhyme.

Repetition of attributions ('says …') in each stanza.

Pupil copymaster

Two more poems

Hi!

Hi! Handsome hunting man
Fire your little gun.
Bang! Now the animal
Is dead and dumb and done.
Nevermore to peep again, creep again, leap again,
Eat or sleep or drink again, Oh what fun!

Walter de la Mare

DONE FOR

Old Ben Bailey
He's been and done
For a small brown bunny
With his long gun

Glazed are the eyes that stared so clear,
And no sound stirs
In that hairy ear.

What was once beautiful
Now breathes not,
Bound for Ben Bailey's
Smoking pot.

Walter de la Mare

(Exemplar alalysis)

Example of analysis of two more poems

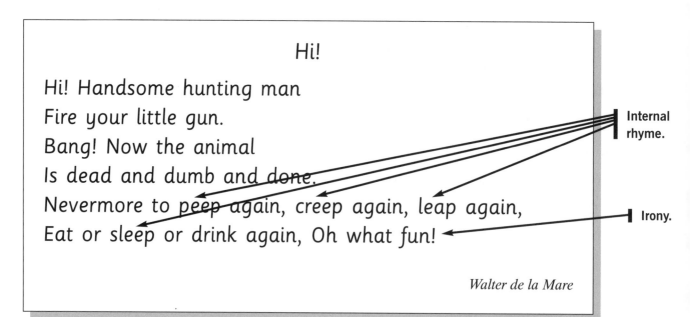

Hi!

Hi! Handsome hunting man
Fire your little gun.
Bang! Now the animal
Is dead and dumb and done.
Nevermore to peep again, creep again, leap again,
Eat or sleep or drink again, Oh what fun!

Internal rhyme.

Irony.

Walter de la Mare

Discussion point: does the poet really mean that hunting is fun? Introduce the term 'irony' (saying the opposite of what you really mean for dramatic effect).

DONE FOR

Old Ben Bailey
He's been and done
For a small brown bunny
With his long gun

Glazed are the eyes that stared so clear,
And no sound stirs
In that hairy ear.

What was once beautiful
Now breathes not,
Bound for Ben Bailey's
Smoking pot.

Walter de la Mare

Discussion point: how does the poet feel about the dead rabbit?

(**Exemplar material**)

Tips to help children memorise poems

Demonstrate how you would approach learning a poem by heart:

- Break the poem into pairs of lines and tackle it a section at a time.
- Work with a partner – you can learn poems most effectively in pairs.
- Say each two lines aloud over and over until they stick in your mind.
- Learn the next two lines.
- Join the bits together.

To help the children further:

- Read the poem on to audio tape. (*An audio tape can be made and shared by the children through a listening station with multiple sets of headphones. This may need adult supervision until a nominated child has mastered the rewind, play and tape counter features of the player.*)
- Ensure that each child has a copy of the poem glued to a piece of card.
- Encourage the children to take the poem home to practise aloud.
- Provide a real audience for performance – this could be the class next door, the whole school in assembly or just the rest of the child's group.
- Encourage the children to use odd bits of time to practise aloud – while changing for PE, on the bus to the pool, walking in line into class, and so on.

Pupil copymaster

Writing frame

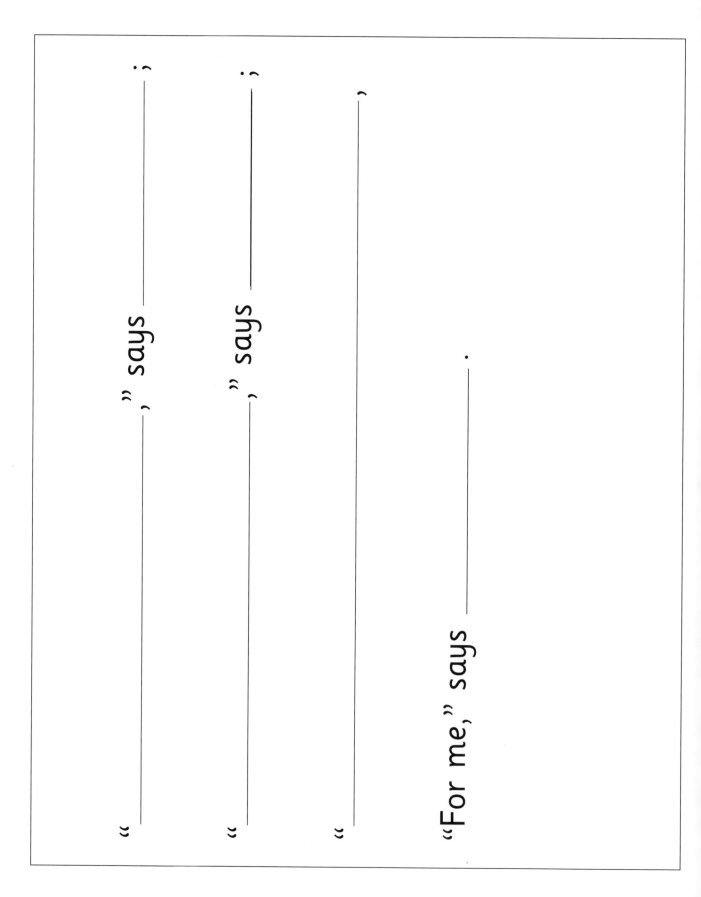

(Exemplar material)

Checklist and model for writing poems

Example of a checklist for writing in the style of Walter de la Mare ①

- Choose a theme for a stanza – favourite food, weather, game, and so on

- Write four lines

- The first three lines start with direct speech

- Follow syllable lengths of model poem for each item

- Repeat names as in model poem, or choose rhyming names of matching length

- The last item should be down to earth and ordinary

Example of modelling a new stanza ②

"Midsummer sun," says Abigail;

"Tropical breeze," says Kareem;

"A loud thunderstorm with a bright lightning flash

"For me," says Dean.

(Marking ladder)

Name: _____

Pupil	Objective	Teacher
	My stanza has four lines.	
	It has a theme.	
	My first three lines start with direct speech.	
	I matched the syllable lengths of the model text for each item.	
	I used the names from the model text.	
	The last item is down to earth and ordinary.	
	How could I improve my poem next time?	

Poems by Tony Mitton

Outcome

A poem written from initial jottings and words; presentation and performance of own or another poem

Objectives

Sentence

2 to read aloud with intonation and expression appropriate to the grammar and punctuation.

Text

8 to read own poems aloud.

9 to identify and discuss patterns of rhythm, rhyme and other features of sound in different poems.

11 to identify and discuss favourite poems and poets, using appropriate terms ('poet', 'poem', 'verse', 'rhyme', etc.) and referring to the language of the poems.

15 to use structures from poems as a basis for writing, by extending or substituting elements, inventing own lines, verses; to make class collections, illustrate with captions; to write own poems from initial jottings and words.

Speaking and listening

● to present and perform own or other poem.

Planning frame

● Own poem shares features with Mitton's *Bubble Songs*:
  - use of first person
  - use of present tense
  - directly addressed to reader
  - use of rhyme
  - use of metaphor
  - use of alliteration
  - use of line beginnings: 'I am …', 'I will …', 'If you …', 'If I …'.

Note

● This unit is based on poems by Tony Mitton, the outstanding modern children's poet. The children will learn one or more of his poems by heart as well as writing their own poem inspired by *Bubble Songs*.

● The outcome for this unit is a step beyond an extra stanza or modelled poem using a writing frame. The children are challenged to take inspiration from the shared text and write their own poems along similar lines.

How you could plan this unit

Day 1	Day 2	Day 3	Day 4	Day 5
Reading and analysis	Reading and analysis Read, annotate and read aloud with expression *Instructions for Growing Poetry* (Resource Pages E and F)	Reading and analysis	Writing	Analysis and performance The children assess poems against marking ladder (Resource Page K) with response partner, polish and perform
Puzzled Pea and *Plum*		*Bubble Songs*	*Writing Our Own Poem*	

Puzzled Pea and *Plum*

Objectives

We will find patterns of words and sound in different poems and read them aloud. We will learn a poem by heart and recite it to an audience

You need: Resource Pages A–D; some pea pods (in case some children have never seen peas except in freezer bags or on the plate!); a plum or other stone fruit.

Whole class work

- Introduce the poem *Puzzled Pea* (Resource Page A) and read it aloud.

- *Who is the 'I' of the poem?*

- *Have you heard the expressions 'alike as two peas' or 'like peas in a pod'?* Show the pea pods to make the point.

- Annotate the poem together (Resource Page B).

- Read the poem aloud together. *What is it that puzzles the pea? Have you ever felt like this?*

- Introduce the poem *Plum* (Resource Page C) and read it aloud.
  - *Who is the 'you' in the poem?*
  - *Who is speaking this time?*
  - *Are there any words in the poem you don't understand?* For example, 'flimsy', 'glum'. 'Flesh' may also be unfamiliar to the children in this context.
  - *What do the last four lines mean?*

- Show the children the fruit with its stone inside to illustrate your point.

- *What would happen if we planted the stone in some earth?*

Independent, pair or guided work

- In pairs, the children annotate a copy of *Plum* (see Resource Page D).

- Allow the children to choose one of the poems to learn by heart ready to perform to a partner, the group or the whole class.

Plenary

- Use the opportunity for performance of the learned poem – try a 'Walk to talk' if the children have been working in pairs. Everyone gets up and moves to find a different partner to share their poem with.

- Ask the children to nominate an especially good performance from another child. This avoids the need to hear 30 performances of the same poem!

- Homework could be to recite the learned poem to someone at home.

Bubble Songs

Objectives

We will find patterns of words and sound in different poems and read them aloud. We will also identify features of poems such as who is the narrator

You need: Resource Pages G–J; whiteboards and pens.

Whole class work

- Introduce the poem *Bubble Songs 1* (Resource Page G) and read it aloud. Ask the children to read aloud the poem with you.

- Give the children 2–3 minutes to quickly sketch what they think is happening in the poem. They show their sketches to a response partner. Identify which pairs have drawn the same picture. Discuss the meaning of the poem.

- As you read the poem aloud again, ask the children to put up a hand if they hear words that have the same sound. Take feedback and then ask volunteers to highlight these words on the display copy of the poem.

- Look carefully at the words in the poem to find sounds that are almost the same – 'wisp', 'gasp' and 'burst'. Explain that these are half-rhymes and are often found in the middle of a group of words rather than at the end of a line.

- Teach through questioning:
  - *Who is the narrator of the poem?*
  - *How many verbs can we find following the pronoun 'I'?*
  - *Who is the person addressed?*

- Discuss other features such as alliteration and the rhythm pattern, and mention the simile (see also Resource Page H).

Independent, pair or guided words

- Read together *Bubble Songs 2* (Resource Page I). Point out the memory-jogging words on the page. Ask the children to use different colours to highlight pairs of rhyming words. *What other features can you see that the poet has used?*

Plenary

- Ask the children what similarities they noticed between the two bubble poems.

- Identify the features with the children – rhyming patterns and sounds in particular.

- Make a class checklist of the features identified (see Resource Page J).

- Ask the children if this would be a poem they would like to keep in the class anthology. What are their reasons for doing so or not doing so?

Writing Our Own Poem

Objective

We will write our own poem from jottings

You need: Resource Pages G, I and J.

Whole class work

- Revisit *Bubble Songs* (Resource Pages G and I) and look at the checklist built in the previous lesson.

- Model writing a new poem (see Resource Page J), and allow the children to assess it against the class checklist.

- Discuss other suitable topics for a similar poem, such as:

> an ice lolly
> a snowflake
> a plastic bag in the wind
> a shirt in a tumble dryer
> a sweet
> a smell (school dinners?)
> a smile
> dust specks in a sunbeam

- When demonstrating writing a poem, model building a generous bank of words and selecting thoughtfully from it. The children are often ready to settle for the first word they think of, especially when rhyming. This can lead to some disappointing results. Encourage them to try different lines, to listen critically and to choose carefully for best effect.

Independent, pair or guided work

- Guided writing sessions with ability groups are the key to success with ambitious topics like this one. Discussion and intervention at the point of planning or writing or polishing will raise the children's confidence and willingness to take risks and experiment with language.

- The children work in pairs to choose a topic and build a word bank, then write independently, turning to their response partners for support if necessary.

Plenary

- Share some good examples with the whole class using a response sandwich: one good comment; one idea for improvement; another good comment.

- The children assess own (or partner's) poems against the checklist.

Pupil copymaster

Puzzled Pea

I'm just a pea
in a plain pea pod.
But there's something about me
that's odd.

For although like the others,
I'm a plain, green pea,
they are all *them* ...
while I'm *me*.

Tony Mitton

(Exemplar analysis)

Example of analysis of *Puzzled Pea*

Rhyme.

Rhyme.

I'm just a pea
in a plain pea pod.
But there's something about me
that's odd.

For although like the others,
I'm a plain, green pea,
they are all *them* ...
while I'm *me*.

Tony Mitton

Rhyme pattern:

A

B

A

B

C

A

D

A

Pupil copymaster

Plum

Don't be so glum,
plum.

Don't feel beaten.

You were made
to be eaten.

But don't you know
that deep within,
beneath your juicy flesh
and flimsy skin,

You bear a mystery.
You hold a key,
You have the making of
a whole new tree.

Tony Mitton

Exemplar analysis

Example of analysis of *Plum*

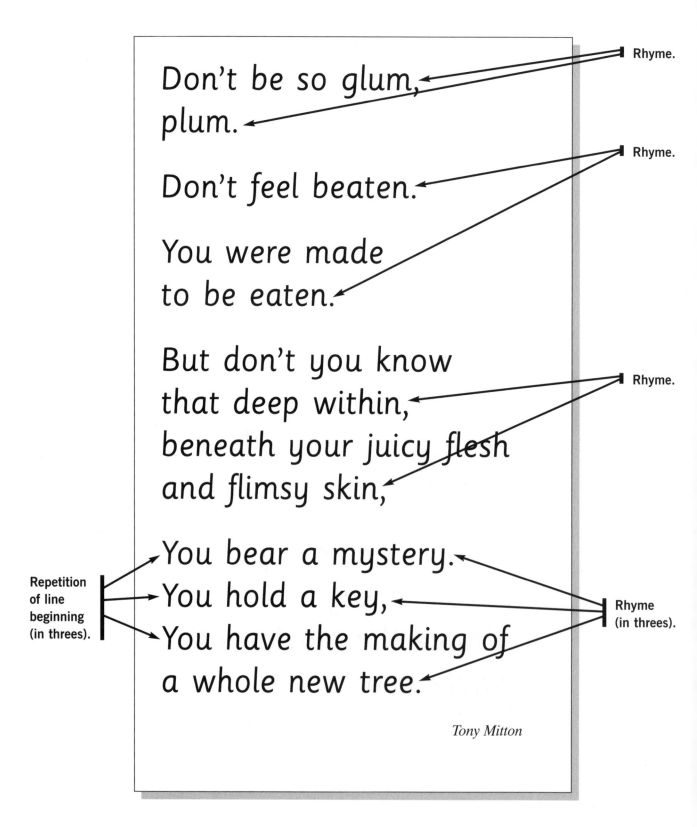

Don't be so glum, plum.

Don't feel beaten.

You were made to be eaten.

But don't you know that deep within, beneath your juicy flesh and flimsy skin,

You bear a mystery.
You hold a key,
You have the making of a whole new tree.

Tony Mitton

Rhyme.

Rhyme.

Rhyme.

Rhyme (in threes).

Repetition of line beginning (in threes).

(Pupil copymaster)

Instructions for Growing Poetry

Instructions for growing poetry
(found on the back of the packet)

Shut your eyes.
Open your mind.
Look inside.
What do you find?
Something funny?
Something sad?
Something beautiful,
mysterious, mad?
Open your ears.
Listen well.
A word or phrase
begins to swell?
Catch its rhythm.
Hold its sound.
Gently, slowly
roll it round.
Does it please you?
Does it tease you?
Does it ask
to grow and spread?
Now those little
words are sprouting
poetry
inside your head.

Tony Mitton

(Exemplar analysis)

Example of analysis of *Instructions for Growing Poetry*

Discussion points: Who is the poet talking to? Why are so many questions asked? What is the answer to them? What metaphor is being used? (seeds = ideas, sprouts = poetry)

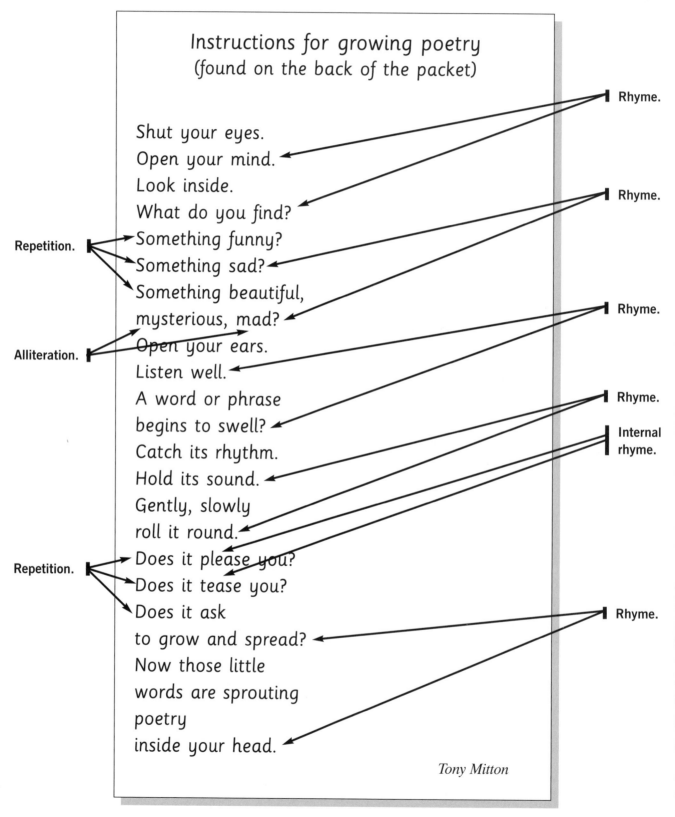

Instructions for growing poetry
(found on the back of the packet)

Shut your eyes.
Open your mind.
Look inside.
What do you find?
Something funny?
Something sad?
Something beautiful,
mysterious, mad?
Open your ears.
Listen well.
A word or phrase
begins to swell?
Catch its rhythm.
Hold its sound.
Gently, slowly
roll it round.
Does it please you?
Does it tease you?
Does it ask
to grow and spread?
Now those little
words are sprouting
poetry
inside your head.

Tony Mitton

Repetition.

Alliteration.

Repetition.

Rhyme.

Rhyme.

Rhyme.

Rhyme.

Internal rhyme.

Rhyme.

Classworks Literacy Year 2 © Sara Moult, Nelson Thornes Ltd 2003

(Pupil copymaster)

Bubble Songs 1

1 If you blow
  I will grow
  to a trembling ball.

  I'm a bubble of breath
  in a shimmering shawl.

  If you lift
  I will drift
  like a wisp of the air.

  Then I'll burst with a gasp
  and I'm simply not there.

  Tony Mitton

(Exemplar analysis)

Example of analysis of *Bubble Songs 1*

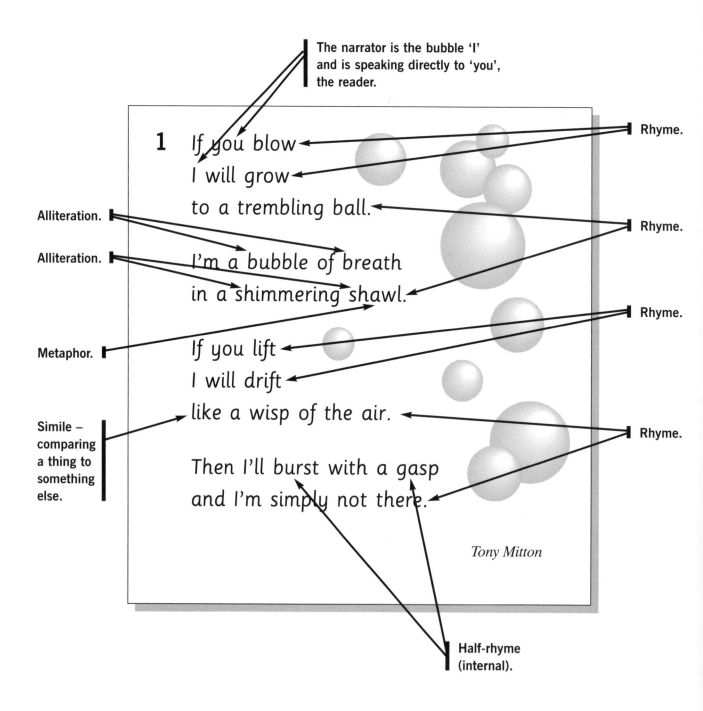

The narrator is the bubble 'I'
and is speaking directly to 'you',
the reader.

Rhyme.

1 If you blow
I will grow
to a trembling ball.

Alliteration.

Alliteration.

I'm a bubble of breath
in a shimmering shawl.

Metaphor.

If you lift
I will drift
like a wisp of the air.

Simile –
comparing
a thing to
something
else.

Then I'll burst with a gasp
and I'm simply not there.

Tony Mitton

Rhyme.

Rhyme.

Rhyme.

Half-rhyme
(internal).

(**Pupil copymaster**)

Bubble Songs 2

2 I am only
a bubble,
The ghost of a ball.
If I'm caught then I'm nought,
I am nothing at all.

I am only,
a bubble,
a shimmering sphere.

If I land on your hand
I shall soon disappear.

Tony Mitton

(Exemplar material)

Checklist and model for poems by Tony Mitton

Example of a checklist for *Bubble Songs*

- Write in the first person ('I')

- Write in the present tense

- Speak directly to the reader ('you')

- Use some rhyming words at the ends of lines

- Use internal rhyme in at least one line

- Use a metaphor

- Use some alliterative words

- Use line beginnings: 'I am ...', 'I will ...', 'If you ...', 'If I ...'

Example of modelling a new poem based on *Bubble Songs*

Johnny Noddy*

I'm just
a reflection,
A trick of the light.

A splinter
of sunbeam
To dazzle your sight.

If you tip
I will dip
And I'll dance on the wall.

But cover your mirror –
I'm not there at all.

* This is what my mother called the dancing reflections inside a room made by shiny objects held and moved in bright sunlight. What do you and the children call them, I wonder?

Marking laddder

Name: _____

Pupil	Objective	Teacher
	My poem is about a non-living thing.	
	It is something that seems to have life.	
	The thing is the speaker in the poem ('I').	
	I used alliteration.	
	I used a metaphor.	
	The end rhymes are _____ .	
	The internal rhymes are _____ .	
	What could I do to improve my poem next time?	

Poetry with Language Play

Outcome

A humorous poem

Objectives

Sentence

1 to read text aloud with intonation and expression appropriate to the grammar and punctuation.

4 to use commas in lists.

Text

8 to discuss meanings of words and phrases that create humour, and sound effects in poetry, e.g. nonsense poems, tongue-twisters, riddles, and to classify poems into simple types; to make class anthologies.

11 to use humorous verse as a structure to write their own by adaptation, mimicry or substitution; to invent own riddles, language puzzles, jokes, nonsense sentences etc., derived from reading: write tongue-twisters or alliterative sentences; select words with care, rereading and listening to their effect.

Planning frame

- 'Top and tail' modelled poem with first and last couplets of model, or adapt rhyming couplets for each new stanza.

- Each rhyming couplet is a silly animal question.

Note

- This unit uses nonsense poems and tongue twisters by various poets to explore some aspects of word play. There is scope for experimentation, with opportunities for writing simple alliterative sentences and performance of poems, as well as the main outcome.

How you could plan this unit

Day 1	Day 2	Day 3	Day 4	Day 5
Reading and analysis	Reading and writing Read *Mrs Rummage's Muddle-Up Shop* (Resource Page E) and *Shop Chat* (Resource Pages G and H). The children write alliterative lists, using commas	Reading and analysis Read *Good Morning, Mr Croco-Doco-Dile* (Resource Page I) and annotate using checklist (Resource Pages J and O). The children read *Ask Jeremy Joe* (Resource Page K) independently and annotate using checklist (Resource Pages L and O)	Writing	Writing The children polish work with response partner using marking ladder (Resource Page P), and learn poems by heart. Perform for partner, group or class
Tongue-twisters			*Silly Animals*	

Tongue-twisters

Objective

We will read, investigate and learn by heart some tongue-twisters

You need: Resource Pages A–D; selected tongue-twisters from school or home; OHT and pens.

Whole class work

- Before the lesson, ask the children to bring along an example of a tongue-twister – in their head or on paper – to share with the class. There are some great examples in the classic musical *Singin' in the Rain*!

- Read *Breakfast for One* aloud (Resource Page A). *How does it make you feel? Hungry?*

- Investigate how the poem has been built (almost mathematically).

- With your class, annotate the poem, tracking the changing positions and forms of the words (Resource Page B).

- *Why is there no punctuation until just before the last line?*

- Practise reading the poem in different ways and at different speeds, for example, with slow relish, dreamily, excitedly and so on.

- *Which reading was most effective and why?*

Independent, pair or guided work

- In pairs, the children read and annotate *Dick's Dog* (Resource Pages C and D).

- The children choose this, *Breakfast for One* or another tongue-twister to learn by heart, working in pairs.

Plenary

- Tongue-twister challenge: who is the fastest and most accurate with their newly learned tongue-twister?

- *What have we learned about how tongue-twisters work?* Answer: use of alliteration, rhyme, rhythm, repetition, oxymoron or comic apposition, nonsense or made-up words, use of humour and so on.

Silly Animals

Objective

We will write a poem modelled on *Ask Jeremy Joe*

You need: Resource Pages K–O; individual whiteboards.

Whole class work

- Revisit *Ask Jeremy Joe* (Resource Page K), and the annotations and checklist from the previous lesson (Resource Pages L and O).

- Demonstrate writing the opening and second stanzas of an alternative version (Resource Page O). Justify your word choices after trying several aloud.

- Make your syllable count very explicit, even letting the children help you so that they grasp the importance of scansion.

- The children assess against the checklist.

- As a class, write a third stanza for *Ask Jeremy Joe*.

- Offer line beginnings for the next stanza and ask the children to complete them on their whiteboards. It may help them to make the silliest word picture they can with each animal.

- Remember to build up a generous bank of rhyming words from which to choose – don't let the children settle for the first to suggest itself.

Independent, pair or guided work

- In pairs, the children produce a word bank, then independently write their own stanzas.

- This work can be differentiated by using either of the writing frames (Resource Pages M and N), or you can encourage some children to write freehand.

Plenary

- The children assess sample poems against their checklist.

- Share-write another stanza or two for the class poem, taking and polishing the best and funniest of the children's work – after getting permission from the poets!

- Reread aloud together with expression.

(**Pupil copymaster**)

Breakfast for One

Hot thick crusty buttery toast
Buttery toasty thick hot crust
Crusty buttery hot thick toast
Crusty thick hot toasty butter
Thick hot buttery crust toast
Toasty buttery hot thick crust
Hot buttery thick crusty toast –

With marmalade is how I like it most!

Judith Nicholls

(Exemplar analysis)

Example of analysis of *Breakfast for One*

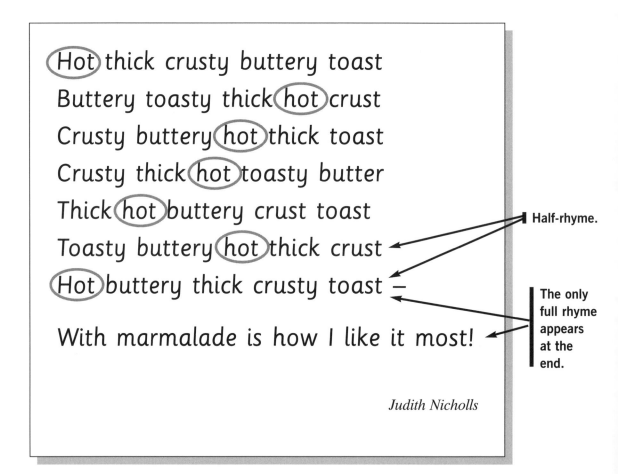

(Hot) thick crusty buttery toast
Buttery toasty thick (hot) crust
Crusty buttery (hot) thick toast
Crusty thick (hot) toasty butter
Thick (hot) buttery crust toast
Toasty buttery (hot) thick crust   **Half-rhyme.**
(Hot) buttery thick crusty toast –

With marmalade is how I like it most!   **The only full rhyme appears at the end.**

Judith Nicholls

The poem uses five words in seven variations. Track changes to word positions and form – for example, '–y' ending, 'buttery' and 'butter'.

Pupil copymaster

Dick's Dog

Dick had a dog
The dog dug
The dog dug deep
How deep did Dick's dog dig?

Dick had a duck
The duck dived
The duck dived deep
How deep did Dick's duck dive?

Dick's duck dived as deep as Dick's dog dug.

Trevor Millum

(Exemplar material)

Example of analysis of *Dick's Dog*

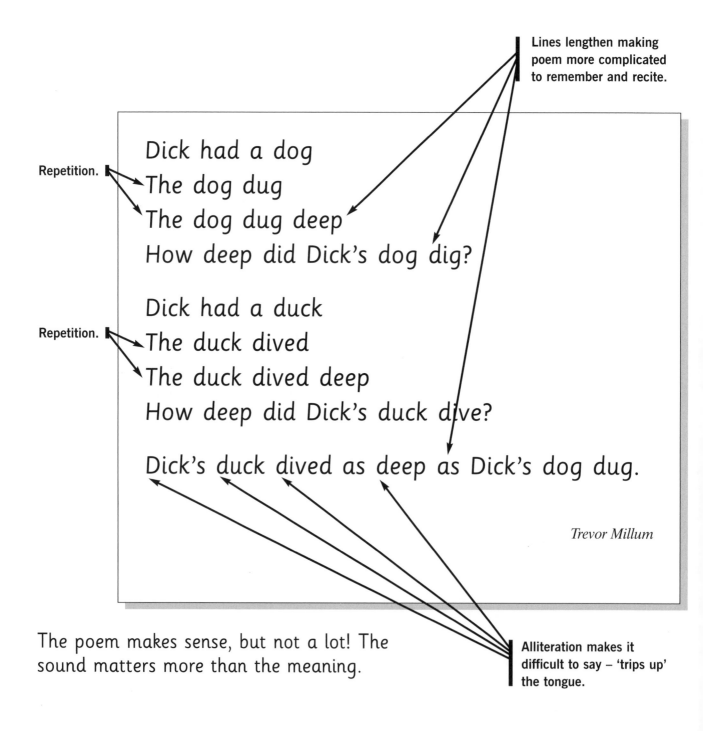

Lines lengthen making
poem more complicated
to remember and recite.

Repetition.

Dick had a dog
The dog dug
The dog dug deep
How deep did Dick's dog dig?

Dick had a duck

Repetition.

The duck dived
The duck dived deep
How deep did Dick's duck dive?

Dick's duck dived as deep as Dick's dog dug.

Trevor Millum

The poem makes sense, but not a lot! The
sound matters more than the meaning.

Alliteration makes it
difficult to say – 'trips up'
the tongue.

(Pupil copymaster)

Mrs Rummage's Muddle-Up Shop

When I tried to ask for a lollipop
in Mrs Rummage's Muddle-Up Shop,
she stopped and said, "I think I might …
"Let's see … I saw one here last night.

"Now, just where did that lollipop go …?
Where exactly …? I don't know.

"Oh dear. This really just won't do …
Is there something else I can get for you?"

And when I said, "I think it's there …"
She just looked blank and scratched her hair.

"Now where," she said, "in a Muddle-Up Shop,
would you go looking for a lollipop?"
And she pulled things out and let them go
As she started to rummage high and low:

"Over here with the diving gear?

"Under there with the underwear?

"Up on top with the soda pop?

"Down below where the loo-rolls go?

"In that box with the fancy socks?

"In this tin with the buttons in?

"Way up high with the rhubarb pie?

"On those racks with the plastic macs?

"By the telly with the raspberry jelly?

"Near the jar where the pickles are?

"Under the stairs with the folding chairs?

"In the bin with the brollies in?"

And she reached up high and she rummaged low
But she wouldn't hear when I tried to show.

"Oh, dear," she'd say, "I'm sure it's here.
How can a lollipop disappear?

"Let's have a really good look around.

That's the way that a lollipop's found …"

It's then I had to shout, "PLEASE STOP!
I JUST WANT TO BUY THAT LOLLIPOP!"

"Oh, that!" she said, "Why goodness me!

You can have that lollipop just for free …

"That is …" she said, with slight distress,

"if you'll help me clear up all this mess …!"

Tony Mitton

(Exemplar analysis)

Example of analysis of *Mrs Rummage's Muddle-Up Shop*

Rhyming couplets.

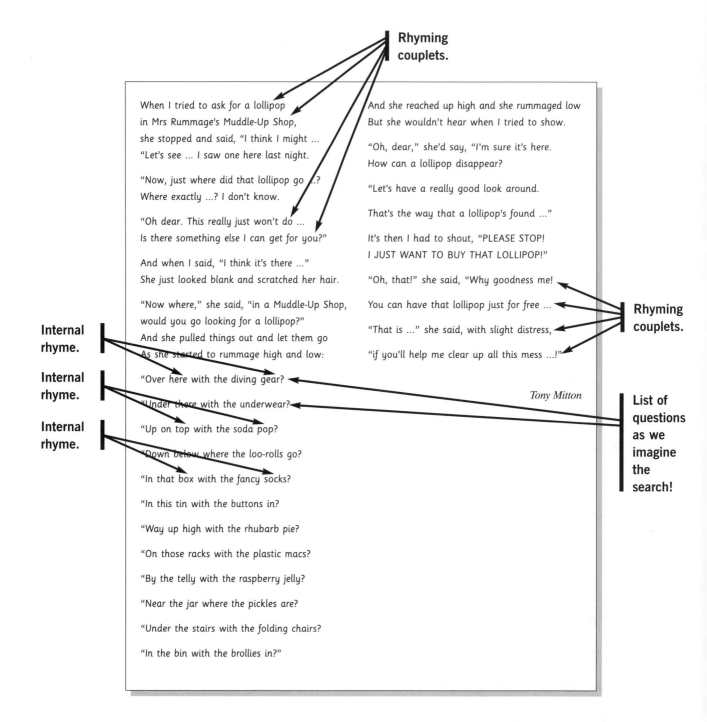

When I tried to ask for a lollipop
in Mrs Rummage's Muddle-Up Shop,
she stopped and said, "I think I might ...
"Let's see ... I saw one here last night.

"Now, just where did that lollipop go ...?
Where exactly ...? I don't know.

"Oh dear. This really just won't do ...
Is there something else I can get for you?"

And when I said, "I think it's there ..."
She just looked blank and scratched her hair.

"Now where," she said, "in a Muddle-Up Shop,
would you go looking for a lollipop?"
And she pulled things out and let them go
As she started to rummage high and low:

Internal rhyme.

"Over here with the diving gear?

Internal rhyme.

"Under there with the underwear?

Internal rhyme.

"Up on top with the soda pop?

"Down below where the loo-rolls go?

"In that box with the fancy socks?

"In this tin with the buttons in?

"Way up high with the rhubarb pie?

"On those racks with the plastic macs?

"By the telly with the raspberry jelly?

"Near the jar where the pickles are?

"Under the stairs with the folding chairs?

"In the bin with the brollies in?"

And she reached up high and she rummaged low
But she wouldn't hear when I tried to show.

"Oh, dear," she'd say, "I'm sure it's here.
How can a lollipop disappear?

"Let's have a really good look around.

That's the way that a lollipop's found ..."

It's then I had to shout, "PLEASE STOP!
I JUST WANT TO BUY THAT LOLLIPOP!"

"Oh, that!" she said, "Why goodness me!

You can have that lollipop just for free ...

"That is ..." she said, with slight distress,

"if you'll help me clear up all this mess ...!"

Tony Mitton

Rhyming couplets.

List of questions as we imagine the search!

(Pupil copymaster)

Shop Chat

My shop stocks:

Locks, chips,
chopsticks,
watch straps,
traps, tops,
taps, tricks,
ship's clocks,
lipstick and chimney pots.

What does your shop stock?

Sharkskin socks.

Libby Houston

(Exemplar analysis)

Example of analysis of *Shop Chat*

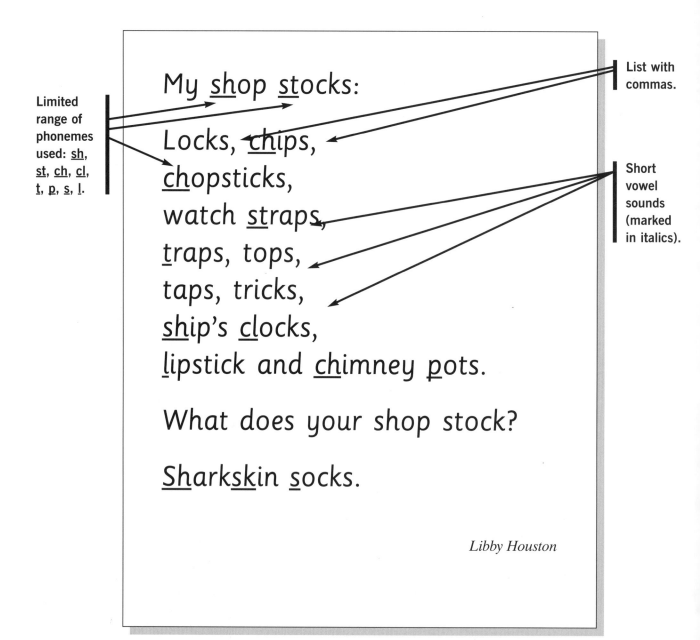

Limited range of phonemes used: sh, st, ch, cl, t, p, s, l.

My shop stocks:

Locks, chips,
chopsticks,
watch straps,
traps, tops,
taps, tricks,
ship's clocks,
lipstick and chimney pots.

What does your shop stock?

Sharkskin socks.

Libby Houston

List with commas.

Short vowel sounds (marked in italics).

Words chosen for sound not sense – but there is some sense, too!
Why not choose a different range of sounds and write a similar one?

Good Morning, Mr Croco-Doco-Dile

Good morning, Mr Croco-doco-dile
And how are you today?
I like to see you croco-smoco-smile
In your croco-woco-way.

From the tip of your beautiful croco-toco-tail
To your croco-hoco-head
You seem to me so croco-stoco-still
As if you're croco-doco-dead.

Perhaps if I touch your croco-cloco-claw
Or your croco-snoco-snout,
Or get up close to your croco-joco-jaw
I shall very soon find out.

But suddenly I croco-soco-see
In your croco-oco-eye
A curious kind of croco-gloco-gleam,
So I just don't think I'll try.

Forgive me, Mr Croco-doco-dile
But it's time I was away.
Let's talk a little croco-woco-while
Another croco-doco-day.

Charles Causley

Example of analysis of *Good Morning, Mr Croco-Doco-Dile*

Good morning, Mr Croco-doco-dile
And how are you today?
I like to see you croco-smoco-smile
In your croco-woco-way.

From the tip of your beautiful croco-toco-tail
To your croco-hoco-head
You seem to me so croco-stoco-still
As if you're croco-doco-dead.

Perhaps if I touch your croco-cloco-claw
Or your croco-snoco-snout,
Or get up close to your croco-joco-jaw
I shall very soon find out.

But suddenly I croco-soco-see
In your croco-oco-eye
A curious kind of croco-gloco-gleam,
So I just don't think I'll try.

Forgive me, Mr Croco-doco-dile
But it's time I was away.
Let's talk a little croco-woco-while
Another croco-doco-day.

Charles Causley

Word play splits the word 'crocodile' and puts a different ending with a matching middle, using alliteration and rhyme.

Rhyme pattern is ABAB throughout.

Ask Jeremy Joe

If you ask a question of Jeremy Joe,
All he will say is, "I don't know!"

Can you brush your hair with a polar bear?
Does a vampire bat wear a bobble hat?

Will a hairy ape eat a purple grape?
Can you catch the flu from a kangaroo?

Can a tiger cub join a football club?
Will a chimpanzee come and dance with me?

You can keep on asking Jeremy Joe
But all he says is, "I don't know!"

(Exemplar analysis)

Example of analysis of *Ask Jeremy Joe*

If you ask a question of Jeremy Joe,
All he will say is, "I don't know!"

Each line is a silly question about an animal.

Can you brush your hair with a polar bear?
Does a vampire bat wear a bobble hat?

Variety of question beginnings keep reader's interest.

Will a hairy ape eat a purple grape?
Can you catch the flu from a kangaroo?

Can a tiger cub join a football club?
Will a chimpanzee come and dance with me?

You can keep on asking Jeremy Joe
But all he says is, "I don't know!"

Rhyming couplets top and tail the poem – tie it together.

Internal rhyme.

Pupil copymaster

Writing frame 1

If you ask a question of Jeremy Joe,

All he will say is, "I don't know!"

Can you _____ ?

Does a _____ ?

Will a _____ ?

Can you _____ ?

Can a _____ ?

Will a _____ ?

You can keep on asking Jeremy Joe

But all he says is, "I don't know!"

Writing frame 2

If you ask a question of Jeremy Joe,

All he will say is, "I don't know!"

_____ polar bear?

Does a vampire bat _____ ?

Will a hairy ape _____ ?

_____ a kangaroo?

Can a tiger cub _____ ?

Will a chimpanzee _____ ?

You can keep on asking Jeremy Joe

But all he says is, "I don't know!"

(Exemplar material)

Checklist and model for poetry with language play

Example of a checklist for writing a poem based on *Ask Jeremy Joe*

- Use a question format

- Use pairs of lines in each stanza

- Use internal rhyme in each line

- Use 10 syllables in each line, rhyming on syllables 5 and 10

- Mention an animal in each line

- Give a silly activity for each animal

- Top and tail with two stanzas about a character

Example of modelling an alternative version of *Ask Jeremy Joe*

If you ask a question of Jennifer Jane
All she will do is say her name.

Can you train a frog to walk your dog?
Will a mountain goat spend a ten-pound note?

Can a tall giraffe take a bubble bath?
Does a lioness wear a party dress?

Will a tiny flea read a book to me?
Can an octopus drive a minibus?

You can keep on asking Jennifer Jane
But she only ever says her name!

Marking ladder

Name: _____

Pupil	Objective	Teacher
	My poem uses the 'top and tail' from the modelled poem.	
	I used a variety of beginnings.	
	I gave each animal a silly activity.	
	I checked my syllable count in each line.	
	I used rhyming words in the middle and at the end of each line.	
	I remembered the question marks.	
	I left a line between stanzas.	
	What could I do to improve my poem next time?	

Traditional Stories from Other Cultures

Outcome

A 'traditional' story modelled on the shared text with a change of setting and characters

Objectives

Sentence

3 to reread own writing to check for grammatical sense (coherence) and accuracy (agreement) – identify errors and suggest alternative constructions.

5 to use verb tenses with increasing accuracy in speaking and writing, e.g. 'catch'/'caught', 'see'/'saw', 'go'/'went' and to use past tense consistently for narration.

Text

3 to discuss and compare story themes.

4 to predict story endings/incidents e.g. from unfinished extracts, while reading with the teacher.

5 to discuss story settings: to compare differences; to locate key words and phrases in text; to consider how different settings influence events and behaviour.

Speaking and listening

- Group story circle to retell story.

Planning frame

- Title modelled on shared text.
  - two contrasting young characters
  - mothers' warnings
  - games they play
  - return home, mothers' reaction and realisation
  - last meeting
  - reflection on what might have been.

Note

- This unit is based on *Why Frog and Snake Can't Be Friends* (available as a big book), a retelling of a traditional Nigerian tale. The story uses colourful and repetitive language and has a strong symmetrical structure. It lends itself readily to adaptations, such as polar bear/seal, mouse/cat, seal/penguin, rabbit/ fox and so on. (Polar bear/penguin is a non-starter – the former only inhabit Arctic regions while penguins are restricted to the Southern Hemisphere.)

How you could plan this unit

Day 1	Day 2	Day 3	Day 4	Day 5
Reading and analysis Read story (Resource Pages A–B) and identify theme	**Reading and analysis** Using storyboards (Resource Pages E and F), the children draw/write three or four key scenes from the story and retell to class in circle, using storyboards as prompts	**Writing** *Planning a Story*	**Reading and analysis** Read story opening (Resource Page A). Annotate, referring to Resource Pages C and J	**Writing** Demonstrate writing story opening. The children use writing frame (Resource Page H) if required and independently write openings

Day 6	Day 7	Day 8	Day 9	Day 10
Reading and analysis Read story middle, annotate using checklist (Resource Page J)	**Writing** Demonstrate writing story middle. The children write middle of story	**Reading and analysis** Read story ending, annotate using checklist (Resource Page J)	**Writing** Demonstrate writing story ending. The children write end of story	**Writing** *Polishing Our Writing*

Planning a Story

Objective

We will plan a story modelled on *Why Frog and Snake Can't Be Friends*, changing the setting and characters

You need: Resource Pages A, B, F and G or big book version of *Why Frog and Snake Can't Be Friends*, by Fraser Williamson (Shortland Publications); flip chart and pens; storyboards from previous lesson; A4 whiteboards and pens, OHTs and pens.

Whole class work

- Skim-read the text again to identify setting (Resource Pages A and B).

- *Where does this story take place? What is special about this setting?*

- *What if the story happened somewhere else? How would we have to change the characters?*

- Demonstrate your adapted storyboard using Polar Bear and Seal in an Arctic setting (Resource Page F). Explain that polar bears hunt and eat seals, waiting at ice holes on the frozen sea where seals come up to breathe.

- Decide on two different activities the animals might play at and teach each other, for example, playing on an icy slope: Polar Bear could roll herself up in a ball and Seal could slide on her tummy.

- Cover up the key speeches for each stage of the story and brainstorm what might be being said in each picture. Then reveal the speech bubbles.

- Gather ideas for different incompatible pairs and match to settings. List them on your board/flip chart.

- The children choose a setting and a pair of characters, then discuss the games they might play with response partners.

Independent, pair or guided work

- The children plan their own story using the storyboard blank and the word bank (Resource Pages G and I), including speech bubbles with key speeches.

- Have several children plan on acetate versions (photocopied later) or have someone on hand to photocopy the children's storyboards onto acetate in time for the plenary.

Plenary

- Share and assess some examples against the original and modelled storyboards:
  - *Has the theme been used?*
  - *What games will the characters play?*

- Invite comments using a response sandwich: one good comment; one area for improvement; another good comment.

- Allow time for the children to highlight any areas they want to improve or amend.

Polishing Our Writing

Objective

We will work with a response partner to read our story through for sense, make any changes and improvements

You need: Resource Pages A–D and K; A4 whiteboards, flip chart and pens.

Whole class work

- Reread sections from the original version of the story (Resource Pages A and B), noting the key features (see the exemplar analysis on Resource Pages C and D).

- Remind the children that their story should follow the shape and theme of the original, even borrowing whole sentences or sentence structures, adapted to fit.

- Together, model writing some sentences from the children's storyboards. You might want to make a few deliberate mistakes so that you can help the children to spot them and then model correcting them. For example:
  - a misplaced 'he', 'she' or 'I'
  - a present tense verb
  - two sentences with a comma splice instead of a full stop between them.

- Correct your work using different coloured pens, neatly crossing through the error.

- Reread for sense when the sentence has been altered and rework if necessary.

- Demonstrate highlighting sentence beginnings or adjectives and verbs that are over-used and replacing them with more varied and interesting choices.

- Isolated correction exercises, especially when there is copying of sentences, are time-consuming and tedious, both for the children and for you marking them. The children rarely make the connection between these exercises and their own writing.

- Let the children scrutinise their own and each other's work for verb agreement, consistency of tense, narrative viewpoint, and so on. If they have watched you model on real text, they will know what to look for and how to correct errors. Response partners and marking ladders used in context are very effective. Consider the difference between the comment you could add to the marking ladder, moving the child on to the next step, and the sort of comment you would write on a completed exercise.

- If some children are finding identifying lapses difficult, plan in a guided writing session to support and scaffold them.

Independent, pair or guided work

- The children work with response partners to proof-read and polish their own stories, referring to marking ladders (Resource Page K). Each child completes his or her own marking ladder and records a comment on their partner's.

- An area for reworking is chosen and tackled if necessary.

Plenary

- *What have we learned and achieved in this unit?*

- Celebrate by the children reading their stories to a new audience.

(**Pupil copymaster**)

Why Frog and Snake Can't Be Friends

Mama Frog had a son, and Mama Snake also had a son. One morning both children went out to play. Mama Snake called after her child, "Watch out for things with sharp claws and teeth that gnaw. Don't lose your way in the jungle, baby, and be back to the burrow before dark."

"Clawsangnaws," sang Snake, as he went looping through the grass. "Beware of the Clawsangnaws!"

Mama Frog called after her son, "Watch out for things that nip or bite. Don't go into the jungle alone, dear. Don't fight, and get home before night."

"Niporbite," sang Frog, as he went hopping from stone to stone. "Beware the Niporbite!"

Snake was singing his Clawsangnaws song, and Frog was singing his Niporbites, when they met along the way. They had never met before.

"Who are you?" asked Frog. "Are you a Niporbite?" And he prepared to spring out of reach.

"Oh, no! I'm Snake, called by my Mama 'Snakeson'. I'm slick, lithe, and slithery. Who are you? Are you a Clawsangnaws?" And he got ready to move, just in case.

"No, no! I'm Frog, called by my Mama 'Frogchild'. I'm hip, quick and happy."

They stood and stared at each other, then they said together, "you don't look anything like me." Just then a fly flew by right past Frog's eyes. Flip! Out went his tongue as he flicked in the fly. A bug whizzed past Snake's nose. Flash! Snake flicked out his tongue and caught the bug. They looked in admiration at each other and smiled. They felt at ease with each other, like old friends.

"Let's play," said Frog. "Since you're not a Niporbite, and I'm not a Clawsangnaws, we could play together."

Frog and Snake started playing games. "Watch this," said Frog. He crouched down and counted, "One a fly, two a fly, three a fly, four!" He popped way up into the air, somersaulted, and came down – whop! "Can you do that, Snake? It's called the Frog-Hop."

Snake slid to a nearby mound to try it. He got to the top of the slope, stood on the tip of his tail and tossed himself into the air. Down he came – flop! – in a tangle of coils. He laughed and tried again.

Then Snake said, "Watch this!" He stretched out at the top of the mound and counted, "One a bug, two a bug, three a bug, four!" Then swoosh! He slithered down the slope on his stomach. "Try that, Frog. It's called the Snake-Slither."

Frog lay on his stomach and slipped down the hill. His arms and legs flailed about as he slithered. He turned over at the bottom of the slope, - blump! – and rolled up in a lump.

All afternoon the two friends slithered and slid and flopped and hopped. Sometimes Snake was best, and sometimes Frog was best. One game led to another and the day sped by. As the sun began to set, the two friends remembered their promise to be home before dark.

"Goodbye," said Snake. "It's been fun." And he gave Frog a big hug. He squeezed him tightly – it felt good to have a friend like Frog. In fact, it felt so good that he squeezed him even more tightly.

"Ow! Easy!" croaked Frog. "Not too tight!"

"Sorry," said Snake, loosening his hug hold. "My, but you feel good, good enough to eat."

Frog laughed. "I like you," he said. "You're my very best friend." Then off they went, frog-hopping and snake-slithering, all the way home.

continued ...

Classworks Literacy Year 2 © Sara Moult, Nelson Thornes Ltd 2003

(**Pupil copymaster**)

Why Frog and Snake Can't Be Friends (2)

When Frogchild reached home, Mama Frog was amazed to see him come slithering in the door.

"Now, what is this, eh?" she said. "Look at you, all covered with grass and dirt. I can tell you haven't been playing in ponds or bogs with the good frogs. Where have you been all day, and what's happened to your legs?"

"Nothing, Mama," said Frogchild. "It's just my Snake-Slither."

At the mention of snake, Mama Frog paled. "Snake? What snake?" she croaked.

"Snake-Slither," said Frogchild. "My best friend, Snakeson, taught it to me today."

"Snakeson," gasped Mama Frog. "Did you say SNAKEson?" Mama Frog trembled and turned a pale green. "Listen, Frogchild, listen carefully to what I have to say." She pulled her son close. "Snakes eat the likes of you and me. They crush you in their coils, they hide poison in their tongues. Snakeson comes from a bad family. You keep away from him, you hear? You be sure to hop out of Snakeson's reach if ever you meet again. And stop this slithering foolishness. Slithering's not for frogs."

Frogchild gulped as he thought of the games he'd played with Snakeson. He remembered Snakeson's hug.

"Now. Sit down and eat your dinner, child" said Mama Frog. And remember, I'm not fattening frogs for snakes, eh?"

Snake, too, reached home. "I'm hungry, Ma," he said, hopping into the house.

"Oh! What a sight you are!" said Mama Snake. "Now where have you been all day?"

"In the jungle, Mama, with my new friend. See what he taught me."

"You look ridiculous," hissed his mother, as Snakeson flipped into the air and flopped onto the ground in a tangled mess. "What new friend taught you that?"

"My frog friend, Frogchild," said Snake.

"Frog? Did you say Frog?" hissed Mama Snake, showing her fangs. "You mean you played all day with a frog and you come home hungry? Now listen, Snakeson, frogs are to eat, not to play with. Frogs are delicious people. Eating frogs is a custom in our family, Snakeson, and hopping isn't. So cut it out, you hear me?"

"But Mama, I can't eat Frogchild. He's a friend," wailed Snakeson.

"Friend or not," said Mama, "next time you meet him, play all you like, but when you get hungry his game is up. Catch him and eat him!"

The next morning Snake was up early. He remembered his mother's words, and the delicious feel of his frog friend when they hugged. He slithered over to Frog's house. "Frogchild," he called, "come and play. My mother taught me a new game, and I'd love to teach it to you."

"I bet you would," called Frog, "but I'm not coming."

"You don't know what you're missing," hissed Snake.

"Yes, I do," laughed Frog, "and I know what you're missing, too."

"Aha!" said Snake. "I see your mother has been talking to you, too." Snake sighed. There was nothing more to say or do, so he slithered quietly away.

Frog and Snake never forgot the day when they played as friends. Neither ever again had that much fun with anybody. Today you will see them, quiet and alone in the sun, still as stone. They are deep in thought, remembering that day of games in the jungle. Both of them wonder, "What if we had just kept on playing together, and no-one had ever said anything?"

But from that day to this, Frog and Snake have never played together again.

Fraser Williamson

$\left(\text{Exemplar analysis}\right)$

Example of analysis of *Why Frog and Snake Can't Be Friends*

Symmetry in the story – similar characters and situations.

Time phrase moves story on.

Mother's warning – hints to the reader about danger.

Mother's warning – parallel with Snake mother (compare wording).

Parallels in their speech – both cautious and suspicious of each other (shown in their words, not directly stated).

Strong verb.

Making friends – shown in their expressions.

Time phrase moves the story on.

Mama Frog had a son, and Mama Snake also had a son. One morning both children went out to play. Mama Snake called after her child, "Watch out for things with sharp claws and teeth that gnaw. Don't lose your way in the jungle, baby, and be back to the burrow before dark."

"Clawsangnaws," sang Snake, as he went looping through the grass. "Beware of the Clawsangnaws!"

Mama Frog called after her son, "Watch out for things that rip or bite. Don't go into the jungle alone, dear. Don't fight, and get home before night."

"Niporbite," sang Frog, as he went hopping from stone to stone. "Beware the Niporbite!"

Snake was singing his Clawsangnaws song, and Frog was singing his Niporbites, when they met along the way. They had never met before.

"Who are you?" asked Frog. "Are you a Niporbite?" And he prepared to spring out of reach.

"Oh, no! I'm Snake, called by my Mama 'Snakeson'. I'm slick, lithe, and slithery. Who are you? Are you a Clawsangnaws?" And he got ready to move, just in case.

"No, no! I'm Frog, called by my Mama 'Frogchild'. I'm hip, quick and happy."

They stood and stared at each other, then they said together, "you don't look anything like me." Just then a fly flew by right past Frog's eyes. Flip! Out went his tongue as he flicked in the fly. A bug whizzed past Snake's nose. Flash! Snake flicked out his tongue and caught the bug. They looked in admiration at each other and smiled. They felt at ease with each other, like old friends.

"Let's play," said Frog. "Since you're not a Niporbite, and I'm not a Clawsangnaws, we could play together."

Frog and Snake started playing games. "Watch this," said Frog. He crouched down and counted, "One a fly, two a fly, three a fly, four!" He popped way up into the air, somersaulted, and came down – whop! "Can you do that, Snake? It's called the Frog Hop."

Snake slid to a nearby mound to try it. He got to the top of the slope, stood on the tip of his tail and tossed himself into the air. Down he came – flop! – in a tangle of coils. He laughed and tried again.

Then Snake said, "Watch this!" He stretched out at the top of the mound and counted, "One a bug, two a bug, three a bug, four!" Then swoosh! He slithered down the slope on his stomach. "Try that, Frog. It's called the Snake-Slither."

Frog lay on his stomach and slipped down the hill. His arms and legs flailed about as he slithered. He turned over at the bottom of the slope, - blump! – and rolled up in a lump.

All afternoon the two friends slithered and slid and flopped and hopped. Sometimes Snake was best and sometimes Frog was best. One game led to another and the day sped by. As the sun began to set, the two friends remembered their promise to be home before dark.

"Goodbye," said Snake. "It's been fun." And he gave Frog a big hug. He squeezed him tightly – it felt good to have a friend like Frog. In fact, it felt so good that he squeezed him even more tightly.

"Ow! Easy!" croaked Frog. "Not too tight!"

"Sorry," said Snake, loosening his hug hold. "My, but you feel good, good enough to eat."

Frog laughed. "I like you," he said. "You're my very best friend." Then off they went, frog-hopping and snake-slithering, all the way home.

continued …

Powerful verbs.

Parallel to Snake's song (compare wording).

Three interesting adjectives.

Another parallel – teaching each other's games.

Time phrase moves the story on.

Powerful verbs.

Hint to the reader of danger – hidden from the character. We know more than Frog does.

Who is doing which action? Perhaps the moves taught by the other.

(Exemplar analysis)

Example of analysis of *Why Frog and Snake Can't Be Friends (2)*

Time phrase moves the story on.

Snake's move.

Reader has to work out her feelings from these verbs – the author doesn't state that Mama Frog is frightened.

Mother's advice and warning in her speech.

Reader has to work out Frog's feelings from these verbs – we are not told he is frightened.

Parallel – mother's advice in her speech.

Frog's move (parallel – they have swapped moves/ actions).

Time phrase moves the story on.

Powerful verb.

Double meaning! The game is eating frogs! Snake thinks Frog doesn't know this. The reader knows that Frog does know.

Parallel – Snake is missing an easy meal – Frog!

When Frogchild reached home, Mama Frog was amazed to see him come slithering in the door.
"Now, what is this, eh?" she said. "Look at you, all covered with grass and dirt. I can tell you haven't been playing in ponds or bogs with the good frogs. Where have you been all day, and what's happened to your legs?"
"Nothing, Mama," said Frogchild. "It's just my Snake-Slither."
At the mention of snake, Mama Frog paled. "Snake? What snake?" she croaked.
"Snake-Slither," said Frogchild. "My best friend, Snakeson, taught it to me today."
"Snakeson," gasped Mama Frog. "Did you say SNAKEson?" Mama Frog trembled and turned a pale green. "Listen, Frogchild, listen carefully to what I have to say." She pulled her son close.
"Snakes eat the likes of you and me. They crush you in their coils, they hide poison in their tongues. Snakeson comes from a bad family. You keep away from him, you hear? You be sure to hop out of Snakeson's reach if ever you meet again. And stop this slithering foolishness. Slithering's not for frogs."
Frogchild gulped as he thought of the games he'd played with Snakeson. He remembered Snakeson's hug.
"Now. Sit down and eat your dinner, child" said Mama Frog. And remember, I'm not fattening frogs for snakes, eh?"
Snake, too, reached home. "I'm hungry, Ma," he said, hopping into the house.
"Oh! What a sight you are!" said Mama Snake. "Now where have you been all day?"
"In the jungle, Mama, with my new friend. See what he taught me."
"You look ridiculous," hissed his mother, as Snakeson flipped into the air and flopped onto the ground in a tangled mess. "What new friend taught you that?"
"My frog friend, Frogchild," said Snake.
"Frog? Did you say Frog?" hissed Mama Snake, showing her fangs. "You mean you played all day with a frog and you come home hungry? Now listen, Snakeson, frogs are to eat, not to play with. Frogs are delicious people. Eating frogs is a custom in our family, Snakeson, and hopping isn't. So cut it out, you hear me?"
"But Mama, I can't eat Frogchild. He's a friend," wailed Snakeson.
"Friend or not," said Mama, "next time you meet him, play all you like, but when you get hungry his game is up. Catch him and eat him!"
The next morning Snake was up early. He remembered his mother's words, and the delicious feel of his frog friend when they hugged. He slithered over to Frog's house. "Frogchild," he called, "come and play. My mother taught me a new game, and I'd love to teach it to you."
"I bet you would," called Frog, "but I'm not coming."
"You don't know what you're missing," hissed Snake.
"Yes, I do," laughed Frog, "and I know what you're missing, too."
"Aha!" said Snake. "I see your mother has been talking to you, too." Snake sighed. There was nothing more to say or do, so he slithered quietly away.
Frog and Snake never forgot the day when they played as friends. Neither ever again had that much fun with anybody. Today you will see them, quiet and alone in the sun, still as stone. They are deep in thought, remembering that day of games in the jungle. Both of them wonder, "What if we had just kept on playing together, and no-one had ever said anything?"
But from that day to this, Frog and Snake have never played together again.

Fraser Williamson

Speaks directly to the reader.

Strong conclusion.

Parallel – both thinking the same. The reader must ask the same question – theme of story is shown here.

Now they both know the truth – the reader works it out from speeches.

Frog and Snake storyboard

Classworks Literacy Year 2 © Sara Moult, Nelson Thornes Ltd 2003

Polar Bear and Seal storyboard

Storyboard blank

1	2
3	4

Writing frame for story opening

Mama _____ had a child, and Mama _____ also had a child. One morning both children went out to play.

Mama _____ called out after her child, "Watch out for _____ _____ . Don't _____ _____ , and be back to _____ _____ before _____ ."

Mama _____ called out after her child, "Watch out for _____ _____ . Don't _____ _____ , and be back to _____ _____ before _____ ."

Word bank

Snake verbs
from the story

looping

sliding

slithering

squeezing

Time phrases from the story

One morning
Just then
Then
All afternoon
As the sun began to set
When ... got home
At the mention of ...
Now
The next morning
Today
But from that day to this

Frog verbs
from the story

hopping

springing

crouching

somersaulting

(Exemplar material)

Checklists for traditional stories from other cultures

Example of a checklist for writing a traditional story

- Use powerful, interesting verbs

- Use time phrases to move the story on

- Include parallels in story: beginning; middle; end

Example of a checklist for writing a traditional story beginning

- Ensure symmetry in the story – similar characters and situations

- Give a clue to the setting in direct speech

- Include mother's warning – hint to the reader about danger

Example of a checklist for writing a traditional story middle

- Making friends – shown in their expressions

- Something in common

- Hint to the reader of danger – hidden from the character. Reader knows more than character does

- Who is doing which action? Perhaps the moves taught by the other

- Mother's advice and warning in her speech

- Reader has to work out character's feelings from powerful verbs

---

Example of a checklist for writing a traditional story ending

- Include a double meaning

- Speak directly to the reader

- Both characters know the truth – the reader works it out from the speeches

- Include a parallel – both characters thinking the same

- Write a strong conclusion showing the theme of the story

Marking ladder

Name: _____

Pupil	Objective	Teacher
	My traditional story uses two similar warnings.	
	I used strong verbs.	
	I used interesting adjectives.	
	My two characters learnt something from each other.	
	What could I do to improve my story next time?	

Word-level starter activities

Vowels and consonants

- Using alphabet cards (a–z), place the vowels face down in a small box and the consonants in another. Invite a child to select two cards from the consonant box and one from the box of vowels. Encourage the children to place the vowel in between the two consonants to create a CVC word. They should then blend the phonemes together to read the word and decide whether it is real or made up.

Which one?

- Write a few spelling variations of a word on the board, for example, 'wos', 'was', 'wass', 'waz'. The children write the correct word and show you. *How do you remember the correct spelling?*

Make a new word

- Write a CVC word on to the flip chart, for example, 'hen'. Invite a child to change one letter to make a new word, for example, 'pen', scribing the new word underneath. Investigate how long a string of words can be created, then begin again with a new start word.

I-spy

- Ask a child to secretly select an object in sight then give its initial letter or phoneme as a clue. The rest of the class should then guess the identity of the object. This game can be extended by giving the final or medial phoneme as a clue as opposed to the initial letter.

Same letter

- The children sit in a circle. Decide on a starting word, for example, 'cat'. Going around the circle, ask each child to add a word that begins with the same initial letter. Extend the activity by going around the circle again with each child adding a word with the same final phoneme or containing the same medial vowel phoneme.

Make a sentence

- Revise the spelling of a consonant digraph, for example, <u>ch</u>, <u>ck</u>, <u>ng</u>. Encourage the children to brainstorm a list of words that use it, and then to create sentences incorporating some of the words collected.

Letter jumble

- Write a CCVC or CVCC word on to a piece of paper, then cut the word up into individual letters. Jumble the letters and challenge the children to unscramble them to identify the original word.

Name game

- Write a selection of the children's names on to a flip chart. Ask the class to identify any words within the names, for example, <u>Car</u>ol, Ju<u>lie</u>, <u>Jam</u>es.

Phoneme pictures

- Hold up an object or a picture of an object. Ask the children to identify the initial/final/medial phoneme, then scribe the appropriate letter/letters on to their whiteboards.

Phoneme search

- Place a variety of objects on the floor, most of which begin with the same initial letter but with a few 'red herrings' added. Hold up a card with the initial letter, then ask the children to identify and collect all the objects beginning with this letter. This game can easily be adapted to focus on hearing and identifying final or medial sounds.

Silly sentences

- Create 'silly sentences' using alliteration. Once given an initial phoneme more able children may be able to work with a partner to create an alliterative sentence, while less able children could complete a sentence begun by an adult. For example, 'Henry the huge horse hated ...'

Make the word

- Give each child a letter of the alphabet. Call out a word, for example, 'car', and ask the children who have a letter necessary to make this word to come out to the front. Once the children have made the word, ask the rest of the class to look carefully at the letter they are holding. If they think they can add their letter to the existing word (for example, 't' to create 'cart') or exchange places with an existing letter (for example, 'n' to create 'can') they should come out to the front and create the new word.

Letters, phonemes, objects

- With the children sitting in a circle, place four letter cards in the centre, for example, 'l', 'm', 'n', 's'. Give each child an object beginning with one of these letters. Ask the children to place their object next to the appropriate letter.

Secret words

- Secretly write a word on the board, then cover it with a strip of card. Reveal the word one letter at a time, asking the children to guess the final word.

Beginnings

- Write the beginning of a word on the board, for example, 'tra'. Invite the children to list on their whiteboards as many words as they can think of beginning with these letters.

Misspelling

- Hold up an object or picture of an object, for example, a doll. Explain to the children that you are going to write the word on the board. Spell the word incorrectly, for example, 'boll', 'don', 'dall', then invite the children to identify which part of the word is incorrect before making appropriate changes.

Robot

- Talk like a Dalek, reading out different words and segmenting each phoneme clearly. Point to children in turn and challenge them to spell the word letter by letter.

Rhyme it

- Write a word on the board. The children have 30 seconds to write as many words as they can that rhyme with this word.

Present to past

- Write a sentence in present tense and ask the children to write it in the past, for example, 'I run' to 'I ran'. Repeat the other way around if appropriate.

Picture it

- This game can be used to help the children with 'difficult' words. Write a word on the board. The children look at it and make a picture in their mind of how the word is written. Seat less-able pupils so they look up to the left of the board. Question the children to build up strategies for the whole class.

Speed writing

- Write a word on the board. Look at it carefully as a class and talk about strategies for learning the word. Give different children 30 seconds to write it on the board as many times as they can.

Car registrations

- Create words from random sets of consonants, for example, from car registration plates. Letters have to appear in the same order as they do on the number plate, for example, RMB – 'remember'.

Sentence-level starter activities

Making sentences

- Put a word on the board, for example, 'dog'. Ask the children to write the beginning of a sentence using this word, for example, 'The dog'. Add another word to the board and ask the children to continue their sentence using this word, then add another, and so on. You can play this on many levels, adding a variety of words, for example, 'shark', 'jelly', 'whispered', 'because', and so on.

Boring sentences

- Give the children a dull sentence to improve, for example, 'The man got out of the car.' Encourage them to rewrite the sentence in a different genre, for example, as a caption, an instruction, a line of poetry, and so on.

Sentence doctor

- Choose a phrase or sentence with a common error, for example, 'He could of danced all night.' Ask the children to be a 'sentence doctor' and 'fix' the sentence.

Imitating sentences

- Write a sentence or part of a sentence on the board, for example, 'Struggling to stay awake, the teachers ...' Ask the children to write their own sentence or phrase using this structure, for example, 'Battling to remain calm, the children ...'

Marking ladder

Name: _____

Pupil	Objective	Teacher
	What could I do to improve my work next time?	